THE EMERGENCE OF BANGLADESH

THE EMERGENCE OF BANGLADESH

Problems and Opportunities for a
Redefined American Policy in South Asia

Wayne Wilcox

American Enterprise Institute for Public Policy Research
Washington, D. C.

Wayne Wilcox is professor of government and research member of the Institute of War and Peace Studies and the Southern Asian Institute, Columbia University. Professor Wilcox began this study while holding a Guggenheim Foundation grant on sabbatical leave from Columbia University, and finished it after having been appointed cultural attaché in the U.S. Embassy, London (on leave from Columbia University). The Guggenheim Foundation, Columbia University, the United States government, and the American Enterprise Institute are not responsible for the views expressed, which are solely those of the author as an independent scholar using public sources.

Foreign Affairs Study 7, September 1973

ISBN 0-8447-3112-9

Library of Congress Catalog Card No. L.C. 73-87975

Printed in United States of America

CONTENTS

INTRODUCTION

The emergence of Bangladesh and the way in which it emerged calls for a fundamental redefinition of American policy toward the states of South Asia.[1] The need for greater clarity of goals in the region is a familiar problem in post-World War II American foreign policy. The initial U.S. role in South Asia seemed to have more to do with the British imperial recession and the fall of Nationalist China than with conditions within South Asian countries themselves. The 1954 Pakistani-American military alliance was part of a global containment doctrine rather than a relationship shaped by regional goals.

Beginning with the Sino-Indian border war of 1962, and continuing through the Indo-Pakistani wars of 1965 and 1971, the regional political relationships of the South Asian states and the global superpowers have been in flux. The emergence of Bangladesh adds another actor to the South Asian stage, but it did little to solidify the regional structures on which might have been built greater cooperation and less conflict-producing tension. Indian regional military hegemony does not, in and of itself, guarantee regional stability.

Neither in 1945 nor in 1973, nor for that matter during the years in between, has there been an American policy consensus within administrations, between Congress and the executive, or between leaders of the two political parties on the main questions posed to Washington by the South Asian situation. These now familiar differences of opinion have been exaggerated by the public debate on the handling of the Bangladesh crisis by the Nixon administration, and by the

---

[1] This need was recognized by President Nixon in his 8 February 1972 press conference when he said: "At this point, we are doing everything we can to develop a new relationship with the countries of the subcontinent that will be pro-Indian, pro-Bengalese, pro-Pakistan but mostly pro-peace." He did not suggest how this was to be done, or over what time period.

1

broader controversies concerning U.S. policy toward underdeveloped countries in general.

The questions raised by a review of American goals, interests and influence in South Asia are unexpectedly numerous. At the most fundamental level, the key problem is posed by the need to address developments within the region and within the states of the region while simultaneously meeting strategic questions involving the region's role in a global context. For the former, decision makers must concern themselves with rather narrow national interests and goals in the economic, social and political life of the various states. For the latter needs, the prime concern must be with the global importance of the region and the posture of American adversaries in South Asia. Policy conflicts are generated by the inability to reconcile regional and global goals, especially during periods in which U.S. doctrine does not assign priorities of attention and resource allocation.

Current U.S. policy in Asia is based on the Nixon Doctrine which is generally thought to counsel limited American involvement, indirect security support for friendly countries, reduced bilateral economic assistance commitments and a "stand down, stand back" local posture. Intrinsic in this position is a commitment to seek greater levels of accommodation with global adversaries and to reduce concern with local centers of conflict.

The difficulty with applying this doctrine in South Asia is that "restraint" or "limited concern" are not policies, that global superpower accommodation does not meet the problems of Sino-Indian, Indo-Soviet, or Indo-Pakistani military relationships, and that South Asian economic and social development cannot be furthered by U.S. "restraint." Moreover, such vague guidelines lead bureaucrats into conflict or paralysis, congressional committees into unsatisfying hearings, and foreign governments into policies reflecting uncertainty about American aims. They also deny an administration the high ground from which to argue for creative policies while encouraging a climate of isolationist or neglectful public opinion. This is not intrinsic in the doctrine enunciated at Guam which principally concerned Northeast Asia and the Indo-China peninsula, but it has had that effect in the absence of policy statements which distinctively recognized and forwarded American goals for South Asia.

This paper concisely reviews past policy goals and modes, to draw some lessons from the Bangladesh crisis, and to advance some ideas for a positive South Asia policy by the United States, one which is compatible with the general guidelines of a less "interventionist" and less security-oriented American posture in the region.

1
UNITED STATES POLICY IN THE INDIAN SUBCONTINENT, 1945-1969

An appropriate policy review must begin with a clear statement of past policies and postures for the obvious reason that history, and memories, weigh heavily upon the present and the near future. This is a particularly valuable exercise for current South Asia policy where myths, partisan arguments, press myopia, classified information, and foreign government lobbying have so thoroughly muddied the waters.

American Asian policy in the twentieth century has attempted to support a balance of power in Asia that would inhibit a successful continental imperialism. The outcome of World War II forestalled Japan's Greater East Asia Co-Prosperity Sphere, while leading to the European colonial recessional. The new threat to an Asia of independent nations was the Sino-Soviet alliance, and by 1950 the cold war had become internationalized. American policy was committed to the support of "anti-Communist" regimes wherever nationalists were threatened. Given America's military hegemony, most Communist regimes or parties opted for nonconventional warfare. In the 1950s, the battlegrounds included Korea, Indochina, Malaya, Burma, Indonesia and the Philippines. In retrospect, most of these conflicts appear to have been more the product of *local* Communist party interests than those of their bloc patrons, but the effect on nationalist regimes and hence U.S. policy was the same.

U.S. declaratory policy from the onset of the cold war to "The Spirit of Camp David" in 1959 was one of comprehensive and consistent opposition to Russian and Chinese foreign policy. The operational consequences of this doctrine included policies directed against the U.S.S.R. and China, and against local Communist parties. These in turn required a "call to arms" directed to new governments in the postcolonial world, and an alliance diplomacy designed to stiffen the confidence and capabilities of third-world governments in facing indigenous and neighboring Communist adversaries.

The Truman and Eisenhower administrations created incentives for *non*-Communist governments to become *anti*-Communist governments. States willing to join vague alliances were offered the protection of American arms, military assistance for their local forces, diplomatic support in regional quarrels (sometimes), and economic assistance. States that desired to stay outside the alliances of the cold war were generally given access to the same kind of resources, but in lesser amounts or of more restricted scope.

In South Asia, Pakistan was a "joiner" and India was a "negotiator." Insofar as the United States had a policy for Nepal,[1] it followed first a "follow-India" and then a "follow-the-king" line—as Nepal sought a balanced position between India and China. With respect to Afghanistan, the United States settled for a position second to that of the U.S.S.R—convinced that Kabul would not ally itself with the United States [2] but that Russian influence could be offset by a modest presence as long as the monarchy lasted. In Burma, after Aung San's assassination by White Flag Communist insurgents, no government was strong enough to have a firm foreign policy. Border troubles with China, overseas-Indian trader troubles with New Delhi, postcolonial xenophobic perspectives on the West, and ethnic, linguistic, and Communist troubles with insurgents left Rangoon with little authority and little room for maneuver. All external powers conducted their policies toward Burma in about the same style—as modest, barely visible efforts to either build up, or tear down, the sitting government.

American policy throughout this region had one object—to foreclose opportunities for the increase of the power of the U.S.S.R., China, and local Communist parties, and where they did exercise influence, to minimize it. In a sense, it was the regional application of a global doctrine, and it appeared to be overzealous given the weak position of U.S. adversaries in the states of the subcontinent. On the

---

[1] This subject is best treated in Leo E. Rose, *The Foreign Policy of Nepal* (Berkeley and Los Angeles: University of California Press, 1971).

[2] There were two factors making for this judgment: First, Afghanistan was the first non-Communist country to receive Soviet assistance in large amounts; and second, Afghanistan and Pakistan had an important boundary dispute. If the U.S. was to have Pakistan as an ally, Afghanistan would not be available, and indeed would have to "reinsure" with the U.S.S.R. But since the close Soviet-Afghan relationship was so early a phenomenon, the U.S. arrival was clearly a late one.

other hand, it was successful, at a low cost,[3] in helping to ensure the maintenance of regimes and regime postures that were supportive of American policy goals. It is arguable that these developments would have transpired anyway, although that argument might be hard to sustain, or that the same goals could have been gained for less. Judgments may differ, but American decision makers in the 1950s pursued this strategy, considering it to be successful and prudent.

The main criticisms of this policy concern the alliance with Pakistan, negotiated late in 1953 and brought into operation in 1954.[4] Critics suggest that the regional consequences of this alliance undercut U.S. global interests in South Asia, that the alliance aligned the United States with an unstable and reactionary government, and that its effect within Pakistan was to undermine economic and democratic development. The critics have tended to be South Asian specialists who viewed the region as unique and peripheral to a global, anti-Communist policy that they might have supported in Europe, the Middle East, or Northeast Asia. Their view was challenged by those who argued that Pakistan was important to U.S. aims in the Middle East, that no region is unique in contemporary world politics, that the alliance connected the CENTO and SEATO alliances, and that the relationship did not, in fact, produce heavy costs in dealing with India, ephemeral public opinion aside.

In retrospect it appears that Secretary of State Dulles and chairman of the Joint Chiefs of Staff, Admiral Radford, decided that Pakistan would be a useful addition to the global alliance system, partly for "bandwagon" effects with Turkey and Iran—Northern Tier countries—and partly for global containment reasons. The price paid for these political gains was military and economic assistance to Pakistan. Military assistance had to be justified in accordance with global doctrine, not diplomatic postures, and therefore officials in Washington were asked to respond to a Soviet "threat" to Pakistan.

Within Pakistan, American alliance assistance came to have three effects: to strengthen the armed services within the political system, to strengthen the central government against other centers of authority in the society, and to strengthen Pakistan against India.

---

[3] Between 1947 and 1970, U. S. assistance to these five states was about $14 billion; the military assistance figures are estimated at about $1.5 billion of this total. *U.S. Statistical Yearbook, 1971* (Washington, D. C.: Government Printing Office, 1971), pp. 759-760.

[4] The alliance was first considered in the Truman administration, but deferred until the 1952 elections and the new administration. See William J. Barnds, *India, Pakistan and the Great Powers* (New York: Praeger for the Council on Foreign Relations, 1972), pp. 86-97.

For Washington, however, arms assistance had three different functions: to cement an alliance, to ensure that the alliance partner was capable of managing its own society, and to add incrementally to Soviet defense problems.

This alliance, like all alliances, changed over time. At the beginning, each partner could overlook the special interests of the other because the relationship had more benefits than costs to both countries. But both governments attempted to change the ratio of obligations and advantages as their own circumstances changed. When General Muhammad Ayub Khan took power in 1958,[5] he began to reduce the level of political intimacy between governments and, after the 1960 U-2 incident and the Sino-Indian War of 1962, he reduced the level of diplomatic cooperation by edging toward normalization first with China and later with the U.S.S.R. Political and diplomatic intimacy were, of course, the highest priority to the founders of the alliance, Dulles and Radford. In the late 1950s, however, the United States came to see the military advantages of Pakistan's location south of the Sino-Soviet frontier as it obtained a base and other useful installations. This neatly reversed the alliance's goals, and made its de facto purpose in 1960 what its de jure purpose had been stated to be in 1954. The alliance arrangements in both cases involved economic and military assistance transfers from the United States to Pakistan in exchange for various levels of access and operation in Pakistan. Between 1954 and 1962, the goals of Washington and Rawalpindi changed but the cost/benefit ratios were acceptable and the vital interests of both parties were served.

In 1962, simultaneously with the Cuban missile crisis, war broke out between China and India along the Himalayan frontier. It appeared to Washington that the Communist states, though divided, had begun to militarize their policies toward third-world states.[6] Once the Russians backed down in Cuba, the United States launched a major assistance effort for India. Although the Chinese had proclaimed a unilateral cease-fire and had withdrawn to their claim lines,

---

[5] He had been, in fact, a power in the state since the early 1950s, and was singularly responsible for U.S. arms assistance.

[6] At the time, some observers believed that the Russian and Chinese steps were coordinated and that the increasing violence in South Vietnam was part of the pattern. More recent research argues for a "coincidental" crisis pattern. In the case of the Sino-Indian border war, both Neville Maxwell in *India's China War* (London: Jonathan Cape, 1970) and Allen Whiting, in a forthcoming book, argue that New Delhi was not the injured innocent it appeared to be at the time, and indeed China believed itself threatened simultaneously by the U.S., U.S.S.R. and India.

India's security appeared to be hostage to China's intentions. Ambassador John Kenneth Galbraith, reporting some years later, observed that the Indian government simply collapsed from within after the shock.[7]

To Washington, the war presented several problems and opportunities. The first problem was to parry the Chinese military threat by transferring weapons and economic resources so that India could build up its own military establishment. The second was to rebuild the Indian government's morale and confidence in its own ability to manage its northern frontier. The opportunities that the war produced were political: the U.S. could greatly increase its participation in India's planning vis-à-vis America's adversaries, the U.S.S.R. and China, and/or it could move New Delhi and Rawalpindi together into an anti-Communist coalition that would serve American global, as well as regional, interests in subcontinental peace. However, it proved impossible to reconcile the approaches to the problems and therefore *both* opportunities were lost.

As soon as military assistance began flowing to India to meet China's threat, Pakistan protested. It argued that the Sino-Indian border clash was small, that India had been most truculent in negotiations, and that the Chinese could not mount and sustain a major cross-Himalayan adventure in India even if they chose to do so. The military assistance India sought, argued the Pakistanis, was in fact directed against them. Efforts to build New Delhi's military confidence would simply lead its officials into a harder line against Pakistan, and the Kashmir dispute would never be solved. Moreover, the assistance would trigger an arms race that would slow the economic development of India and Pakistan unless a "deal" on Kashmir was made a prerequisite to military aid to India.

The U.S. and Britain sent a joint mission to the subcontinent to attempt to reconcile the local parties' views of their needs. Led by Averell Harriman and Duncan Sandys, the mission tried to reconcile the Indian and Pakistani positions, while assessing India's military needs and attempting to conciliate Pakistan. It was unsuccessful, perhaps more unsuccessful than its leaders knew. The public airing of diplomatic confusions, especially between Mr. Sandys and Mr. Nehru, was incredible. The Indians felt that they were being blackmailed by Pakistan through the Western countries when Indian survival was at stake, while the Pakistanis felt that the Indians were cleverly using a little adversity to gain immense new military re-

---

[7] *Ambassador's Journal: A Personal Account of the Kennedy Years* (Boston: Houghton Mifflin Co., 1969).

sources. The U.S. and British governments were attempting to minimize their own costs in arming India, while maintaining Pakistan's support. If only the Chinese had "returned from Elba" to re-create a sense of crisis, perhaps a settlement could have been produced. As it was, no one was satisfied.

U.S. and British military assistance was more limited than the Indians had hoped. When the Indian request for large numbers of high-performance American aircraft was not met, the Indians turned to the U.S.S.R. for supply. Moscow was eager to forestall the anti-Communist opportunity that the Sino-Indian War had opened.[8] In a somewhat confused but finally precedent-breaking policy, the U.S.S.R. agreed not only to sell India high-performance aircraft, but to build plants in India for their manufacture.[9] By 1964, whatever opportunity the United States might once have had to bring India into a special defense relationship was lost and, even more important, the U.S.S.R. had begun to develop such a relationship.

However, American and British military assistance to India was much greater than Pakistan had hoped it would be, given the absence of a Kashmir settlement, and the government of Pakistan began to turn to China and the U.S.S.R. for aid to offset the changes in the subcontinent. The standard Russian history of the period, I. M. Kompantsev's very candid *Pakistan i Sovetskii Souiz* (1970), notes that 1963 was a "breakthrough" year in Soviet-Pakistani relations. The oil and gas exploration agreement first signed in 1961 was extended, a Karachi-Moscow air route agreement was signed, the government of Pakistan "dropped its unreasonable positions" with respect to trade and Russian access to the country, and a Pakistani-Soviet cultural association was formed.

Pakistan's more important initiatives, however, were with Peking. A frontier agreement was negotiated and signed, and Peking endorsed Pakistan's position in the Kashmir dispute. Trade and credit agreements were established, and military assistance discussed. There was a marked increase in missions from one country to the other, and Pakistan International Airlines was given a much sought after route

---

[8] The Russian formulation on the war was as follows: "In what position did the Soviet Union find itself? Its ally—though unfaithful still an ally—was invading a country which was bound to the U.S.S.R. by strong friendly relations. . . . China was aware of the U.S.S.R.'s relationship with India. . . ." Cited in David Floyd, *Mao Against Khrushchev* (New York: Praeger Publishers, Inc., 1964), p. 366.

[9] See Ian C. C. Graham, "The Indo-Soviet MIG Deal and Its International Repercussions," *Asian Survey*, vol. 4 (May 1964), pp. 823-843, for a detailed analysis and chronology of the negotiations.

to Canton and Shanghai.[10] These steps worsened Pakistani-American relations and further weakened the opportunity for creating a détente between India and Pakistan, whether by bilateral or by third-party mediation. Moreover, the previous close cooperation between Washington and Rawalpindi on global military problems was also lost.[11] The beneficiaries of these setbacks for the U.S. were the U.S.S.R. and China.

This trend, or set of parallel unhappy accidents, was sealed in the 1965 Indo-Pakistani War. The roots of the war lay in three factors: the peculiar problems of President/Field Marshal Ayub Khan in Pakistan's political system, the apparently weak regime of Lal Bahadur Shastri in India, and the weakening relative military position of Pakistan. There was a national, indirect election in Pakistan in 1965 in which the opposition illuminated many of the mistakes and venalities of Ayub Khan's government. While Ayub won the election (with some help from his police and administrators), he found himself greatly undermined, if not wholly discredited, as a national figure. He needed a spectacular success of some sort, and events in Kashmir in 1965 suggested that he might be able to gain it by reopening the issue through a localized military operation.

Lal Bahadur Shastri had inherited a shaky Indian government after the Sino-Indian War and Nehru's death. His image, inside and outside India, was that of the modest mediator cast in the Gandhian mold. In the Rann of Kutch, a contested territory which is little more than a salt marsh, Ayub Khan tested Shastri's will in a limited battle in the spring of 1965. Pakistan's army did well, and India's government accepted international mediation of the dispute. Ayub Khan may have imagined that India would do the same in Kashmir, completely misreading the effect of the Rann of Kutch affair in Indian domestic politics, and especially in civil-military relations within the Shastri administration.

A final factor driving Pakistan to war was the beginning of a major Indian buildup, underwritten quite modestly by U.S. and British aid, but quite considerably by Soviet sales and development commitments (including support for a major Indian arms production program). If Pakistan was to reopen the Kashmir dispute by force

---

[10] For a detailed study, see my chapter "China's Strategic Alternatives in South Asia," in Tang Tsou, ed., *China in Crisis*, vol. 2 (Chicago: University of Chicago Press, 1968), pp. 395-431, which lists agreements, missions, and other dimensions of the growing Sino-Pakistani relationship.

[11] Even though the U.S.-Pakistan bilateral treaty was secretly renewed in 1964, according to Dr. G. W. Choudhury (conversation), the Pakistan government closed the Peshawar base in 1969 to accommodate the U.S.S.R.

of arms, it had to do so immediately, or so Ayub Khan and his advisers thought.

The war was fought in September 1965 on the approaches to Kashmir and along the West Pakistan-India frontier. The military result was a stalemate, which meant a Pakistani political defeat. The magnitude of the loss was unforeseen because Pakistan badly miscalculated the American response.

At the outset of the war, the United States had announced an arms embargo applicable to both sides and had suspended all shipments of military and economic assistance. The Indians bitterly complained that the villain and the victim were subjected to the same punishment, but it was Pakistan that felt the full brunt of the policy. The latter's economy was heavily dependent upon American economic assistance, and its military forces were almost entirely equipped with American arms. It had no alternative sources of supply and very little foreign exchange with which to buy. In a limited war of attrition, it could last about two months.

After military reverses, Ayub Khan attempted to invoke American mediation that might yet produce some useful benefit. President Lyndon Johnson, who was then deeply concerned with the developing Vietnam War and its demands on American resources and patience, told him to take his case to the U.N. When the Russians offered to mediate at Tashkent, Pakistan, lacking any other choice, accepted the offer, as did India, and the war ended. The status quo ante bellum formed the terms of the Russian-arranged settlement, and Ayub Khan was forced to accept what for him was the political *coup de grace*. His foreign minister, Z. A. Bhutto, shortly thereafter left the cabinet and took the "surrender" to the streets. Ayub Khan responded with repression, and a country that had found some reason in the 1965 elections for doubting his probity and neutrality came to see him as a blundering, antipatriotic tyrant. He was to last until March 1969, when he was toppled from power in disgrace.

American policy during and after the war disappointed both India and Pakistan, propelling India into greater dependence upon the U.S.S.R. and Pakistan into much closer relations with China. While U.S. economic assistance, mainly loans, continued to be forthcoming and indeed remained a crucial factor in the development of both countries in the 1960s, it was not accompanied by a clear American doctrine for South Asia. Washington had become agnostic about the strategic value of India and Pakistan, and its eroding interest in these countries was confined to economic growth objectives. Subcontinental cynics attributed this to American commercial interests, while American well-wishers attributed it to humanitarian values and technocratic momentum.

After 1965, U.S. military assistance policy suffered from the absence of focus. Certain "nonlethal" items were made available for sale following the war, but other arms sales were prohibited. The main policy question turned on the definition of "nonlethal." This led to such ridiculous fictions as labelling a munitions factory for India as nonlethal, while allowing Pakistan to buy some ammunition and spare parts on the same grounds. Policy guidelines that force such strained interpretations testify to the absence of policy.

India and Pakistan both realized that military equipment would have to come from other sources and spent heavily from funds that might otherwise have been invested in economic growth. Pakistan bought in France (Mirage aircraft), Italy (small submarines), the U.S.S.R. (helicopters, trucks, tanks), and China (tanks, MiG-19 aircraft, an ammunition factory, small arms). India continued its large purchases from the U.S.S.R. (submarines, Petya class destroyer escorts, patrol boats, Su-7 fighter-bombers, MiG-21s and helicopters—both Mi-4 and Mi-8).

Soviet assistance to Pakistan, both diplomatic and military, came at a price to the United States. At the U.S.S.R's request, Pakistan was to close the American facility at Peshawar and reduce cooperation in other ways. It probably bargained with the U.S. before doing so, but finally acceded to Soviet demands in exchange for modest support. China's aid was also impressive—MiG-19s and tanks—and had the same adverse effect on the attitude of the American government without in any way appreciably offsetting Indian strength.

By 1969 the levels of American influence and access in South Asia had declined markedly as Chinese and Soviet influence appreciably increased. Despite about $10 billion in economic assistance to India, including special food shipments to tide her over the bad crop years of 1964-66, Washington was seen to be either hostile to or unconcerned with India's political and strategic future. And despite $830 million in military assistance and about $4 billion in economic assistance to Pakistan, American leverage in that country was very modest. The ravages of the Vietnam War had emasculated the U.S. commitment to a "decade of development"; the national consensus favoring an interventionist foreign policy for America had evaporated; and India and Pakistan seemed remote and peripheral to the great issues troubling the domestic scene. U.S. policy was not only unfocused, it was disspirited.

2
THE COLLAPSE OF PAKISTAN'S POLITICAL SYSTEM

The late 1960s brought hard times to South Asia. India suffered severe food shortages occasioned by three poor monsoon seasons. The closure of the Suez Canal had deprived Indian industry of traditional markets and sources of supply and had increased freight costs. The military costs of recruitment, development and deployment were high. Foreign exchange remained very dear, dependent as much on the International Bank for Reconstruction and Development Aid-India Consortium as on the policies of the government of India. India's political life was also unsettled: Lal Bahadur Shastri died in Russia after signing the Tashkent agreement, and Mrs. Indira Gandhi was struggling with her "elders and betters" for control of the Congress party and the cabinet. When the party split over Mrs. Gandhi's insistence upon leadership prerogatives, observers inside and outside India prophesied the end of stable governments and an era of weak coalitions.

In Pakistan, the economic picture was better but the political picture was worse. After Tashkent, Ayub Khan and his cabinet decided to finance the army buildup by levying higher taxes and by cutting all "social overhead" capital investments. The finance minister told his friends that Pakistan could not afford to be sentimental, that public health, welfare, education and social facilities would have to wait upon the needs of the garrison. Directly productive capital investments were to continue—in part to justify World Bank and U.S. levels of assistance and in part to take care of the constituents of the weak and failing government—in other words business groups, large farmers, import-export traders and the praetorian guard. This strategy squeezed the uninfluential public three ways—through increased taxation, increased inflation, and decreased services. The repression required to keep the government in power did not allow elections or referenda to determine if the people thought this strategy to be in the interests of Pakistan's defense or of their grandchildren's future. They were told that this was necessary, and they soon observed that sacrifice was more necessary for some than for others.

The Fall of Ayub Khan

This policy had dire effects on popular support, and more and more coercion was necessary to maintain order.[1] Ayub Khan's health also began to deteriorate, and two assassination attempts were made on his life before the regime finally collapsed in the winter of 1969. During the whole of this period, Pakistan's foreign policy was bravely advertised by its managers as a successful U.S.-U.S.S.R.-China "triangular tightrope" walk. The imagery is more telling than was intended, since Pakistan had nowhere to go but down, and staying aloft on thin wires pulled by outsiders was the essence of the act.

The collapse of the Ayub Khan regime had a politically cathartic effect within Pakistan. But trade unions, in a wave of euphoria, demanded wage increases of several hundred percent. Younger men in the civil and military services imagined that, with their corrupt or inefficient superiors purged, they would be captains of the ship. Provincial politicians and leaders believed that the collapse of Ayub Khan signalled the end of the special powers of the central government, and they looked forward to greater autonomy and freedom of maneuver. The press and intelligentsia hoped that a less repressive regime would permit them to return to centers of influence. The army had come to consider Ayub Khan to be an embarrassing liability—more a political than a military leader and, after Tashkent, more interested in political survival than military strength.[2]

Outside the country, the relief was also immense. The staff of Harvard's Development Advisory Service, who had worried about the lack of social investments, could hope that the new regime would be more "distributionist" than "expansionist." U.S. AID staff members would feel less inhibited in defending aid to Pakistan if the government were more representative.

---

[1] This pattern of arrests for "political and group" offenses has been brilliantly used by Shahed Javed Burki to show the decline of the Ayub Khan regime in West Pakistan. See his forthcoming *Social Groups and Political Development: A Case History of Pakistan* (Cambridge: Harvard University Press).

[2] For a description of the environment, see Lawrence Ziring, *The Ayub Khan Era: Politics in Pakistan, 1958-1969* (Syracuse, N. Y.: Syracuse University Press, 1971); David Loshak, *Pakistan Crisis* (London: Heinemann, 1971); and L. Rushbrook-Williams, *The East Pakistan Tragedy* (London: Stacey, 1972).

Yahya Khan Attempts to Hold Pakistan Together

The martial law regime that replaced Ayub Khan was weak. Yahya Khan was barely *primus inter pares* in the general staff, and his own interests and capabilities were not those of a master politician. In the immediate aftermath of his take-over, he attempted to use his military colleagues as paternalistic reformers. The aroused populace would not have it, and civil-military and interservice rivalries were too intense for this approach to work as an administrative system. The "whiz kids" brought to Islamabad to reform the system made uncoordinated, contradictory proposals, and found themselves outvoted.

Yahya Khan reluctantly concluded that the country would have to be returned to the parliamentarians, at least in part. He announced nationwide elections on the basis of the adult universal franchise, and somewhat later issued a Legal Framework Order (LFO) which was to create an interim structure of authority and constitutional boundaries within which parties could contest the elections. This order, promulgated on 30 March 1970, had five major points: (1) the country should be a federation, the unity of which "is not in any manner impaired"; (2) the constitution must provide for Muslim ideology, democracy, civil rights, and the independence of the judiciary; (3) the provinces should have maximum autonomy within the needs of the federal government to "discharge its responsibilities in relation to external and internal affairs, and to preserve the independence and territorial integrity of the country"; (4) the people of all parts of the country should be full participants in all national activities; and (5) "within a specified period, economic and all other disparities between the provinces and between different areas in a Province are to be removed by the adoption of statutory and other measures."[3]

Yahya Khan's declarations made it clear that he recognized the legitimacy of East Pakistan's economic grievances against the West,[4] an issue that had emerged as the country's most massive problem *after* Ayub Khan's fall. In almost all dimensions of national life, Bengal was second best. In 1947, East Bengal—Muslim Bengal—had

---

[3] The Legal Framework Order, 30 March 1970, Article 20, reprinted in *Federal Intervention in Pakistan—Chronology*, Information Division, Pakistan Embassy, Washington, D. C., p. 13.

[4] These are treated most carefully, and most comprehensively, in Rounaq Jahan's *Political Integration and Political Development in Pakistan* (New York: Columbia University Press, 1972). A less reliable, though oft-cited source, is "Conflict in East Pakistan: Background and Prospects," by E. S. Mason, R. Dorfman and S. Marglin (Harvard University unpublished paper, April 1971).

joined Pakistan but was the poorest part of Bengal, with the lowest percentages of urbanization, industrialization, literacy, electrical power capacity and per capita income. Its voice in national politics was weak—in the first seven years of independence because refugees from India ran the national government, and in the next fifteen years because the (West) Pakistani army ran the government. Its slight numerical majority in the electorate ran directly counter to its inferior role in both the political and administrative spheres.

Moreover, the leaders of the country were insensitive to Bengal's needs and aspirations, and their few efforts to integrate Bengal more closely into national life were clumsy. This process of disintegration had begun when the country's leaders declared that Pakistan would have one official language, Urdu, a language which only 8 percent of the population of East Pakistan spoke or read. Riots and shootings in Dacca in 1952 reversed the policy, but not the damage. To scorn Bengal's culture and language and to deny Bengalis a decent place in political and administrative life was as obtuse as it was divisive.

The issue that was dramatized as central in the conflict was economic disparity. This was a serious problem, but it was important principally because it was a clear, unambiguous indicator of political neglect.[5] Economic disparity had the virtue of being easily stated: the per capita income differential between the two wings of Pakistan could be shown to represent not only absolute differences but also trends indicating that things were getting relatively worse for the East. In 1959-60 per capita income was 32 percent higher in West Pakistan than in the East; in 1969-70, it was 61 percent higher. Bengalis were told by their provincial leaders not to accept as satisfactory the absolute growth in the East, but to note the interprovince "gap"; not to consider the fact that per capita income figures are a frequently misleading indicator in economics, because they dramatically showed Bengal disadvantaged. East Bengal was certainly not treated equitably. But such slogans did not contribute to balanced public debate because they did not relate to Bengal's low starting point, its extreme development problems, or the distribution of economic resources in investment and consumption by the private sector.[6] Indeed, more than one observer has noted that Bengal's difficulties were as much the product of the Pakistani class system as the nature of the federal union or of public policy.

---

[5] It was unambiguous to the degree, at least, that economic problems can ever be.

[6] For a concise study of the economic pattern, see J. J. Stern and W. P. Falcon, *Growth and Development in Pakistan, 1955-1969* (Cambridge, Mass.: Harvard, Center for International Affairs Paper 23, April 1970).

The decisive evidence of discrimination is the pattern of government expenditure. There can be no doubt that the national government of Pakistan was not even-handed, let alone partial, toward East Pakistan at any time in the nation's history. Some economists would reckon the internal (East to West) transfer of resources to have been about $2.5 billion between the periods 1948-49 and 1968-69. That is a large figure. Moreover, what it represents is capital not available for the East Pakistan provincial government to spend on social services. The skewing of foreign economic and military assistance,[7] which saw the West utilizing $520 million, the East $128 million, and common projects $132 million in the period 1949 to 1961 (thereafter the breakdown was somewhat more equitable), also contributed to growing disparity. One can debate the fine points of this issue for a long time.[8]

The facts of the matter were that West Pakistan had a more favorable investment climate, both because of labor and infrastructure, than the East; that it therefore attracted a group of Indian Muslim entrepreneurs who made their main investments there and who were aided in doing so by foreign aid and Pakistani government policy; and that this kind of growth fed on itself, as is so notable in developing countries,[9] to Bengal's relative disadvantage.

It was not, therefore, economic disparity that produced the conflict between the two wings of Pakistan, but the conflict that produced the issue of disparity. The issue ran counter to any effective West Pakistan strategy of managing East Pakistan dissent—it could not be denied, and was not denied—and ran parallel to deeper political and cultural conflicts that would have been difficult to manage even in its absence. In any case, Yahya Khan imagined that there might be a political solution to this cluster of grievances in the outcome of a general election. For his part, he apologized for discrimination in the past, and did so early—July 1969—in his administration.

At this juncture, the United States government was hopeful that a peaceful return to democracy could occur, that the issue of disparity in foreign assistance could be corrected by a major U.S. effort to emphasize aid for East Pakistan projects and that the new constitution

---

[7] According to the Mason, Dorfman, Marglin paper, "Conflict in East Pakistan."

[8] This is done for the West Pakistani side of the argument most comprehensively in Rushbrook-Williams, *The East Pakistan Tragedy*, pp. 106-116; on the East Pakistani side by Jahan, *Political Integration and Development*, passim.

[9] Every economist since Nurkse has understood that industrial development creates the conditions for its own expansion by an intense spatial concentration of the factors of production, which in turn minimizes transport, marketing and skill costs.

would provide the basis for continuing national union. The actions of AID and the words of many advisers in reshaping the Pakistan program, however, convinced some Pakistanis that Americans were actively backing secessionists in Dacca.

Election Strategy and National Union

The election campaign began in earnest in late summer 1970. In September, there was massive flooding in East Pakistan and the elections were postponed until 7 December. This extension was criticized by the provincialist (Bengali) Awami League—and exploited as well, since the longer the election period, the greater the chance that the league could reach out beyond its city strongholds in East Pakistan. There was also criticism of the relief efforts of the government, though it was mild compared to what was to follow. On 12 November a massive cyclone and tidal wave struck East Pakistan with devastating force. In this catastrophe, the government was widely charged with callous indifference to the fate of the villages and peoples affected, and this became the "final proof" of the neglect the people of East Pakistan had suffered. It was the Awami League which was to benefit, overwhelmingly, from the charge that "nothing was done, because we are Bengalis." From the few unbiased accounts available, it seems clear that little was done for the victims, but only because there was little with which to do it.[10] The coastal districts have no communications links with the district capitals, and there were no vehicles, boats or helicopters immediately available with which to ferry the meager stockpiles of medical and food supplies. But the press and public relations handling of the crisis by the Yahya Khan regime was disastrous.

Fifty-three million Pakistanis went to the polls on 7 December 1970. On average there were five candidates for each of the 300 seats, and twenty-five parties were entered in the competition. In East Pakistan, the Awami League won 167 national assembly seats of the 169 allocated to East Pakistan and swept the provincial elections, winning 268 of 279 seats. In the West, Z. A. Bhutto's Pakistan People's party won 81 of 143 assembly seats allocated to West Pakistan. The outcome of the election was never in doubt, but the

---

[10] An excellent eyewitness account is Dom Moraes, *The Tempest Within* (New Delhi: Vikas, 1971). Moraes, the son of a famous Indian editor, had no axe to grind. His reports show that relief efforts depended overwhelmingly on the people involved, whether Bengali or non-Bengali, most of whom were trying their best with few resources and less information.

magnitude of the Awami League victory was remarkable. Bengalis had exercised their infrequently given right to indicate their displeasure.

Later in the same winter, India went to the hustings as well. In an equally dramatic and convincing win, Mrs. Gandhi's faction of the Congress party swept the polls and she was returned with a comfortable majority in the national parliament. India's economic position was also improved, with a "green revolution" producing much more grain, and with good rains in 1969 and 1970 laying the basis for widespread agricultural growth. The dislocations of defense expenditures and foreign trade changes had been successfully mastered, and there was an air of optimism about a country that twelve months earlier had been genuinely troubled.

The Failure of Accommodation Attempts

Between 7 December 1971 and 25 March 1972, Pakistan's political leaders looked for a basis for cooperation that would not sacrifice the interests of their constituents or their own position with their followers. The Legal Framework Order of March 1970 posed nearly irreconcilable goals: provincial autonomy but national integration, economic parity between and within provinces, but the maintenance of "sufficient" national armed forces.

The position of Sheikh Mujibur Rahman, leader of the triumphant Awami League, appeared to be the strongest but was in fact the weakest. He was the unlikely leader of a broad provincial coalition, representing almost every shade of opinion and contention. Any major compromise which he made to produce a constitution would have cost him a segment of his coalition before the constitution was approved. And while Mujib probably understood the necessity for compromise, how was he to justify it to an electorate that had given him such an overwhelming mandate and still remain the great consensual figure in a divided society?

The Awami League leaders knew, however, that they had to come to an understanding with the army (and therefore with the major West Pakistani politicians) or risk civil war. Some members of the Awami League openly argued for East Pakistani independence, no matter what the cost, while others believed that real autonomy would allow later independence if the settlement did not prove to be advantageous. Mujib sought to walk a fine line, pressing for the maximum amount of provincial autonomy that any of his followers could demand, while avoiding a breakdown of talks and the precipitation of a civil war. He rested his negotiating position on the so-called six points.[11] They were: (1) a federal, parliamentary, adult franchise democracy; (2) a national government restricted in jurisdiction to defense, foreign affairs and, to a degree, currency; (3) monetary independence of the currency managers for both wings; (4) fiscal policy administered by the federating units, with federal finance the product of provincial agreement; (5) separate provincial foreign economic policies, including aid negotiations; and (6) para-military forces maintained by provincial governments "to contribute effectively toward national security."

During the period of negotiation, there was a great feeling of euphoria in East Pakistan.[12] Bengali nationalism had been expressed, its leaders were meeting West Pakistanis on the high ground for a change, and there was general agreement that "we have won." Nirad Chaudhuri, writing somewhat sourly about his fellow Bengalis, noted at the time that the election and its aftermath

> has a set pattern which demonstrates the truth of the saying that in democratic politics the satisfaction of a pride is infinitely more important than the satisfaction of an interest. . . . So if a burning passion, positive or negative, remains unappeased in an electorate it will always sway votes without any reference to the soundness or the practicality of the mandate given by the voters.[13]

In such a climate, it was not unnatural that non-Bengalis would feel the boot and the lash. This was particularly true of the "Biharis," Urdu-speaking refugees who had fled India in 1947 and had modestly prospered in East Pakistan.[14] They had become local symbols of West Pakistani dominance and were known for their anti-Indian and anti-Hindu views. Their relative wealth and influence was both visible and vulnerable in their shops. There was some looting and some killing, not because the Awami League ordered it or because the

---

[11] Reprinted in L. Rushbrook-Williams, *The East Pakistan Tragedy*, pp. 117-118.

[12] And assertion as well. See Rounaq Jahan, "Elite in Crisis: An Analysis of the Failure of Mujib-Yahya-Bhutto Negotiation" (Harvard University unpublished paper, 19 March 1972), for a description of the radical wing of the Awami League and its militarization.

[13] *Hindustan Standard*, 31 December 1970.

[14] The numbers of these refugees are disputed. Eight percent of the population of East Pakistan claimed literacy in Urdu in 1951, a group of about 5.5 million. This would have included the indigenous Bengali Muslim elite as well as refugees. Since 1951 there has been some emigration to West Pakistan, but also population growth. Some Biharis have become wholly Bengali. Estimates of the size of the Bihari community in Bangladesh in 1973, therefore, range between 1 million and 5 million.

army condoned it, but because law and order had started to weaken, leaving to the mercies of hoodlums a previously protected but alien privileged group.

The more radical of the Awami League's followers condoned this savagery as "overdue justice," even though Mujibur Rahman condemned it and attempted to stop it. The same faction of the party managed to heap scorn on all West Pakistanis, including the troops and their families. A thousand miles separated a West Pakistani soldier from reinforcements of his kith and kin, and young Awami League militants reminded soldiers of that fact. Emotions ran high. Mujibur Rahman found himself attempting to negotiate while many members of his coalition were doing everything possible to provoke a showdown leading to independence.

Yahya Khan's position was no happier and no stronger. He had issued the Legal Framework Order, had acknowledged the result of the elections, and had publicly announced (in Dacca, on 14 January 1972) that Mujibur Rahman would be the country's next prime minister. Yet he found himself with an Awami League that would not compromise on matters of national unity as he demanded. Even if he had been willing to accept a confederation, it was by no means clear that he could win the support of the army—for such an agreement would have spelled an effective end to that same army.

As the crisis deepened, Yahya Khan's dependence upon a consensus within the general staff also deepened, and he found himself a captive of his senior colleagues. Moreover, it became clear by late spring that the majority of the army's officers believed they would have to intervene if the Awami League rigidly held to a literal translation of the six points into a constitution. Generals Hamid and Umar appear to have been the major figures in holding Yahya Khan's policy firm on the "central powers and taxation" issue.

The third major factor in the constitutional bargaining was West Pakistan, represented by the somewhat shakily ensconced Z. A. Bhutto. His electoral victory was much less impressive than Mujibur Rahman's and, for many of the seats he carried, his margin was narrow. On the other hand, he was perhaps the most skillful and certainly the most experienced politician at the "high table." Because his mandate was ambiguous, Bhutto had to *become* the spokesman for West Pakistan in the talks, and therefore he took a constitutional line which was much more "regionalist" than his electoral campaign had been. What would be the effect on West Pakistan, he asked, if there was an army-Awami League deal? Many West Pakistani politicians had privately stated that they thought West

Pakistan would do well to give the East its walking papers—that it was a liability and would be a greater one if it had 55 percent of the seats in the national assembly.

Bhutto's posture was ready-made. The Awami League would have to deal with him or West Pakistan would simply separate from the East. At worst, that would leave him the chief leader of a nation of 55 million; at best, it would make him the king-maker of a country of 120 million. The danger, however, was that the army would reach an agreement with the Awami League at the expense of the richer provinces of West Pakistan and that Bhutto would be leader of the opposition, faced with the legislative majority of the Awami League and the military power of the army. This forced Bhutto to take the position that the constitutional order had to be mutually agreeable to him and Mujibur Rahman.

The trouble with the negotiations was that all three major leaders were weak. Not one of them could accept what would have had to be a major, visible compromise without being rejected by their followers. As a result, each group made its irreconcilable demand and committed all of its resources in the hope that they would be enough. This left Mujibur Rahman with the position of "national hegemony or provincial secession," Bhutto with the position of "shared national power or West Pakistan secession," and the army with "adequate support for national unity and defense or civil war."

The timing of the crisis leading to the outbreak of hostilities stemmed from the fact that the Legal Framework Order had provided 120 days after an election for the constituent assembly to sit and adopt a constitution. Several versions of a constitution were in circulation, with the key sections on state finance and provincial-federal relations left blank. By February, however, the negotiating parties were deadlocked and the Awami League was demanding that the assembly sit on 3 March to write the constitution (on the basis of the league's majority, of course). On 15 February Z. A. Bhutto threatened to boycott the assembly unless he and Mujib reached a compromise on the hard issues before the assembly sat. In short, he would not allow the Awami League (solely on the basis of its majority) to write the constitution.[15] On 1 March Yahya Khan honored Bhutto's request and announced the indefinite postponement of the assembly. On the same day, Yahya removed Admiral S. M.

---

[15] On 27 February Z. A. Bhutto requested that Yahya Khan postpone the National Assembly meeting, promising attendance at a later date if the 120-day minimum drafting period deadline was lifted. Bhutto's case is argued in his *The Great Tragedy* (Karachi: Pakistan People's Party, 1971).

Ahsan, a popular figure, as governor of East Pakistan. Mujibur Rahman responded on 2 March by calling a remarkably successful general strike in East Pakistan. Press censorship was reimposed in East Pakistan by martial law authorities and Pakistan International Airlines began continuous flights of army forces to Dacca.

On 3 March Yahya Khan retreated a step, calling a meeting of all parties in Dacca for 10 March. Mujibur Rahman refused to accept Yahya's response to Bhutto's *diktat,* and something like an independent government started to function in East Pakistan. On 6 March Yahya Khan retreated further, announcing that the assembly would meet 25 March but, at the same time, indicating that he was "pledged to preserving the absolute national integrity of Pakistan." All sides had escalated.

On 7 March Mujibur Rahman responded to the president's speech with four demands: (1) the immediate end of martial law, (2) the army to be returned to its barracks, (3) the establishment of an inquiry into army shootings during the general strike, and (4) the immediate transfer of power to elected representatives. Until these conditions were met, the people of East Pakistan were asked not to pay taxes (starting 8 March) and to close all government offices and universities to show West Pakistan's leaders that East Pakistan was united behind Mujibur Rahman. In response, Lieutenant General Tikka Khan, reputedly the best combat general in the army, was appointed governor and martial law administrator on 9 March, but an East Pakistani judge refused to swear him in.

Bargaining between the Awami League and the army, representing a now more unified West Pakistan, was becoming ever more violent. The army had been moving more troops into East Pakistan to meet any contingency, while the Awami League was paying mind to its defense as well by relying upon the support of the police, the East Pakistan Rifles, and various border security units, but mainly on the unity of the Bengalis. General strikes, the Bengali-Bihari-West Pakistani tension, the confusions of curfews, and army action had led to many deaths.

The last visible effort to produce a settlement was Yahya Khan's 15 March trip to Dacca.[16] He was accompanied by a prestigious working committee, including a former chief justice. Discussions took place on two levels, between the principals and between the working staffs. By this time, Dacca had the appearance of a separate country, and a "Bangladesh" flag had been designed. By 21 March

---

[16] On the same day, however, Mujib issued thirty-five directives taking over the civil administration in the name of Bangladesh.

other West Pakistani leaders, including Bhutto, were in Dacca to be involved in the settlement. Lesser party leaders from West Pakistan returned home the next day and told the press that the army and the Awami League had arrived at a settlement.[17] Bhutto stayed behind, and Mujibur Rahman declared Pakistan Day—23 March—to be "resistance day." At 11 P.M. on 24 March Mujibur Rahman's chief negotiator, Tajuddin, declared that no further talks would be held. On the evening of the 25th, Yahya Khan flew west, and the war began.

During this whole period foreign embassies were reporting on the developing situation, but no decisions were being made that affected outcomes. The United States was formally neutral, but its officials on the spot were very divided. There was no policy, and so there was a struggle for policy. Within a month of the carnage of 25-26 March the U.S. consul-general in Dacca and several of his staff had been transferred, and U.S. policy toward Bangladesh and the insurgency had become "noninterventionist," implying support for national union. But on the night of 25-26 March it was a settling of old scores between the taunted army and the taunting Bengalis, between the peasants of the Punjab and the shopkeepers of Dacca and Chittagong, between West Pakistani Muslims and hated Bengali Hindus and their friends. Nirad Chaudhuri had proven prophetic in his 31 December 1970 article. "The fanaticism which exists in West Pakistan may seek practical satisfaction by coercing any movement in East Pakistan which may be called secessionist, if it is balked in its desire to act on India."[18]

Whom the army considered to be its enemies in the university, in the Awami League, and in the press were attacked with large caliber weapons. The lives of prominent Hindus were forfeit. The real fighting was between the army and the East Bengal Regiment, police, and frontier forces.[19] The terrible effect of an army out of control, convinced of the wisdom of its killing and looting, was made

---

[17] The Karachi stock market share prices rose appreciably, even though Yahya Khan announced the indefinite postponement of the National Assembly meeting scheduled on 25 March.

[18] *Hindustan Standard*, 31 December 1970.

[19] Colonel M. A. Q. Osmany, commander-in-chief of the Mukti Bahini, told an interviewer after the war that "If the Pakistanis had only limited their action against selected politicians, Bengalis in the army and the police might have stayed neutral. . . . The Mukti Bahini was manufactured overnight by the Pakistani army." Khushwant Singh, "Freedom Fighters of Bangladesh," *Illustrated Weekly of India*, 19 December 1971, p. 22, cited in M. Ayoob and K. Subramanyan, *The Liberation War* (New Delhi: S. Chand, 1972), p. 123.

worse by its official pietism. At the end of the first week, the army's Tikka Khan could look at the depopulation of the cities and the flight of the intellectuals and feel assured that Bengalis were not fighters. Z. A. Bhutto aligned his party with the army's action on 27 March. The civil war had become full-blown, but it looked like a walk-through for the Pakistani army after its first month.

3

THE ROAD TO
INDIAN INTERVENTION

The Indian government, like most governments, was taken by surprise by the events that followed 25-26 March. The first wave of refugees, largely mobile and well-trained members of the elite, was welcome "proof" to the Indians of the bankruptcy of West Pakistan's military masters. It supported all of India's views on Pakistan.[1] While West Bengal suffered from many of the same disabilities as East Bengal, developments after March brought a new excitement to Calcutta. Mujibur Rahman became something of a regional folk hero, made all the more poignant by his imprisonment. Tajuddin Ahmad, Mujibur's *chef de cabinet*, arrived in India to set up a government-in-exile and to direct world opinion to the injustices being perpetrated in Bangladesh. The wave of spontaneous Indian public support was telling, and governmental support, begun in the United Nations on 29 March, was also considerable, although quietly given. After all Pakistan had done to embarrass India in Kashmir and in the Naga and Mizo Hills, it must have been sweet satisfaction for New Delhi to return the favor.

The Civil War: First Phase

At the beginning of the insurgency, little Indian military assistance seemed necessary. Mujibur Rahman had appointed his own military adviser, former Colonel Usmani (or Osmany), and there was no doubt that after the army attacks on the East Bengal Regiment, the East

---

[1] After the Indian victory, Mrs. Gandhi explained events in a broad philosophical way, relating them to the 1947 partition: "The war with Pakistan and the emergence of independent Bangla Desh had falsified the two-nation theory and vindicated our principle of secularism." *Indian and Foreign Review*, 1 February 1972.

Pakistan Rifles, the Border Guards and the provincial armed police were pro-Awami League. They had weapons, military training, and access to communication and transportation equipment. In addition, they knew where the arms stores were kept, and how to get at them.[2] It has been charged that there was some Indian complicity in this affair before March, but there has been no verification of this. Even if there was such Indian involvement, it must have been modest compared to the core of "Mujib's army," the regular forces of Bengalis that had been under West Pakistani command in the province.

The government of Pakistan's "White Paper on the Crisis in East Pakistan" (Ministry of Information, 5 August 1971) argues that the Awami League had a "battle plan" calling for the following military steps: (1) the seizure of airports and ports to stop the landing of West Pakistani troops, (2) the isolation or capture of West Pakistani troops in the cantonments of the province, and (3) occupation of key posts on the Indian frontier to facilitate the receipt of assistance. The West Pakistani paper further argues that the plan was to go into effect on 26 March and that the Awami League counted upon Indian assistance if the battle with West Pakistani troops was extended.

There is no way to independently confirm the existence of such a plan, but nothing in it is illogical. If Mujibur Rahman and his associates understood the problems of bargaining with the army and the risks of civil war, as they surely did, they could hardly have neglected a counter-strategy. Their one hope was to isolate the West Pakistani garrisons, deny them reinforcement, and eliminate their threat to an Awami League government. Given the general feeling of optimism in the period between December and March, and the fact that the East Pakistanis under arms were pro-Bengali, but most importantly that they represented a unified people, the Awami League leadership had every reason to imagine that this was an adequate contingency plan. India's prohibition against Pakistani air over-flight, begun after the hijacking of an Indian civil airliner on 30 January, as well as the long distances involved in ocean resupply, gave the Awami League every advantage if a short conflict did develop.

This military situation was surely as obvious to the West Pakistani garrison commanders and Yahya Khan as it was to the

---

[2] L. Rushbrook-Williams, whose research was certainly aided by the government of Pakistan, suggests that Mujib's military planning was much more advanced than has been generally assumed, that there was a "revolutionary army" command standing by in case of war, that retired servicemen were tapped for action, and that arms supplies were being built-up in India close to the frontiers for the East Pakistani forces' use. *The East Pakistan Tragedy*, pp. 66-67.

Awami League, and this was the reason for reinforcing the West Pakistani forces in the province.[3]

In the military as in the political field, there was an escalation of postures and capabilities. Almost from the beginning, the Pakistani army considered India to be deeply involved in the security problem. India's moral and political support for the Awami League, its policy of banning overflights and attempting (unsuccessfully) to get Ceylon to do the same, and its frontier "sanctuary" policy appeared to be key factors in the Awami League's militant posture. It would have been unnatural if the Awami League had not courted Indian support for this purpose, but that did not make it less galling to the West Pakistani commanders.

The war that developed on the night of 25-26 March was very complex.[4] The main struggle was between the West Pakistani garrisons and the armed forces of the East Bengal Regiment, the East Pakistan Rifles and the Border Guards/police. Very limited press reporting from the balconies of the Dacca Intercontinental Hotel and Dacca University almost entirely missed this point. Most of the violence was not directed against the unarmed—although as part of a policy of intimidation in the major cities, some of it certainly was—but rather against "Mujib's army." There have been no reliable casualty figures, since "deaths" became a weapon of psychological warfare in the insurgency that followed, but it seems clear that most of the early dead were soldiers. A large segment of the Chittagong garrison was killed by East Pakistani forces, while the discovery of mass graves in Comilla shows that the West Pakistani garrison there killed large numbers of East Pakistani forces. Certainly the first and most important battles of the civil war were fought when West Pakistani troops attempted to disarm or destroy their former comrades in arms, presumably because they were seen as hostile whether this was the case or not.

The first phase of the war was won by the West in about three weeks, due to superior communication, weapons, and organization. But it is also true that casualties were very heavy, and the "victory," such as it was, was limited to the main towns and resupply points. At this point the West Pakistani army numbered only about 60,000

---

[3] The press reported that six troop ships with 10,000 soldiers aboard landed in Chittagong and Khulna on 25 March.

[4] Reports at the time discussed the interplay between the general strike, military efforts to move cargo and supplies, "mutiny" and disarmed garrisons, great insecurity of military families and very badly disrupted communications due to industrial strikes. It must have been extremely difficult for all sides, distant from the capital, to know the precise nature of the political developments.

in a province of about 60 million. Authority in the countryside was either with the Awami League or nonexistent, and the normal banking, marketing, and tax collection of the national administration disappeared. Most of the junior members of the civil administration were Bengalis who either took flight to India or took up arms with the guerrillas. A large number of the best-trained members of the military and civil services went to India for sanctuary, and subsequent action as a government-in-exile.

In the first phase of the war, sporadic guerrilla activity was largely focused on the destruction of communications and transportation lines to deny mobility to the West Pakistani forces. General Tikka Khan, always publicly optimistic about the restoration of central government authority, admitted that the damage was very great: "If the entire population works hard, we hope to accomplish this (reconstruction) in one year." [5] Yet in the same breath, he said that the military situation throughout East Pakistan was completely under control. (This meant that Bengali forces no longer threatened Pakistani military positions, but not that authority of the central government had been restored.)

The International Reaction

Throughout the spring, Pakistan was under very great international pressure to accommodate the legitimate demands of the Bengali people, to reduce the level of coercion, and to begin immediate rehabilitation and restoration of destroyed facilities. Mrs. Gandhi's formulation of the problem found wide support in the world. This was a case, she argued, of "the historical upsurge of 75 [sic] million people of East Bengal," whose elected leaders had been arrested and whose fellow countrymen had been killed by the thousands. More importantly, she said that India could not help but be affected by this development, and hence it could not stand by passively.

President Podgorny of the U.S.S.R. addressed a strong plea for a "political settlement" to Yahya Khan, noting that the Bengali people's elected leaders could not rightly be denied their voice in Pakistan's future. He also called, as did most foreign governments, for humanitarian assistance for the victims of the conflict. [6] U.S. pro-

---

[5] Quoted in the *New York Times*, 7 May 1971.
[6] This message is reprinted at the end of the article by Deshpande in Ayoob et al., *Bangla Desh: The Struggle for Nationhood* (New Delhi: Vikas, 1971), pp. 128-129.

nouncements were low-key, stressing humanitarian concerns, but U.S. action was quite vigorous. In April, the United States embargoed all arms shipments to Pakistan. To do this, it stopped the issuance of new licenses or license renewals for munitions, "placed a hold" on the delivery of foreign military sales items, and "held in abeyance" any consideration of an October 1970 "one time exception" sales offer. Under this policy, however, Pakistan was allowed to receive arms and munitions which were already being shipped or which had been acquired and were awaiting shipment. From March to October 1971, the value of shipments in these categories amounted to $3.8 million.[7] The clear policy signal to Pakistan was that the United States was unwilling to either sell or grant military assistance for use in the civil war but it was also clear by that time that the U.S. was not pursuing goals of a divided Pakistan.

On the economic assistance front, International Bank of Reconstruction and Development policy reflected American views. Its technical team reportedly argued against new economic assistance to the Yahya Khan regime as long as the civil war continued, especially in light of Pakistan's unilateral debt moratorium steps. Key advisers to Robert McNamara of the World Bank were being pressured by many American leaders and groups to embargo all aid except that for refugees and the rehabilitation of East Pakistan.

Pakistan experts outside government also made vigorous efforts to interest both the administration and Congress in steps designed to force West Pakistan's leaders to negotiate a settlement with the imprisoned Mujibur Rahman. The Mason, Dorfman, and Marglin paper of April 1971, "Conflict in East Pakistan: Background and Prospects," previously cited, was widely circulated and, although hastily drafted, had a significant impact. Senator Edward Kennedy's subcommittee on refugees put the matter on the agenda of Congress, and by May the Senate Foreign Relations Committee reported out a resolution that would have made any government (Pakistan) using military assistance against its own people (East Pakistan) "immediately ineligible for further assistance."[8]

Peking, much to the consternation of the Awami League and to the surprise of many observers, completely backed the Yahya Khan

---

[7] U.S. Department of State, Bureau of Public Affairs, "U.S. Military Supplies to Pakistan," *GIST*, no. 60 (October 1971). In February 1972, congressional sources suggested that the amounts were considerably larger because of "surplus stock" in *overseas* depots having been shipped in a routine manner. Critics of American policy charged that this was a deliberate deception, not bureaucratic oversight.

[8] Senate Congressional Resolution 21, cosponsored by 19 senators.

regime. It charged Indian interference and noted that the civil strife was part of the internal affairs of Pakistan.[9]

In Islamabad, the government of Yahya Khan was asking for time, not support. The army appeared to think that it could reestablish a credible authority within three months, that the Awami guerrillas would be a minor force, and that the world would accept the fact of another stillborn Biafra. Its main concern was with India, because as the army forces pushed against the guerrillas, Indian sanctuaries became increasingly important. Border districts became depopulated simply because the fighting had moved to them, and with Indian protection of the guerrillas, the battles were inconclusive. The government of Pakistan welcomed the idea of observers and refugee assistance teams on the frontier, but the Indian government for equally obvious reasons banned them.

The Civil War: Second Phase

By June, the pattern of fighting had changed. East Pakistani regular forces had been largely suppressed or forced into India, the remaining Mukti Bahini guerrillas had shifted to a strategy of sabotage in the cities and interior, and direct military action was concentrated in the border districts. The Pakistani authorities in the East began granting travel permits to journalists and businessmen. In July, the Indian army took over the border areas from the para-military Border Security Forces.[10]

The focus of the struggle for what would become the new country of Bangladesh moved to the international arena, and to the top of the agenda of the Indian government. Large numbers of refugees had moved into neighboring Indian states because of the fighting. The initial trickle of the elite had been followed by a flood of ordinary peasants. Moreover, the Pakistani forces had begun to re-create an administration in the province, relying heavily upon the

---

[9] The phrasing was relatively vague. "The revelant measures taken by President Yahya Khan in connection with the present situation in Pakistan are the internal affairs of Pakistan; in which no country should or has the right to interfere. . . . The Chinese Government and people will, as always, resolutely support the Pakistan government and people in their just struggle for safeguarding national independence and state sovereignty and against foreign aggression and interference." New China News Agency, 11 April 1971, reprinted in Ayoob et al., *Bangla Desh: The Struggle for Nationhood*, pp. 130-131.

[10] This is discussed with great sophistication by Ayoob and Subramanyan, *The Liberation War*, pp. 167-168.

Urdu-speaking Bihari community of "loyalists." This led to even greater refugee flight, especially among the East Bengali Hindus, who had been suspected of collusion with India. This put the Indian government in a still greater quandary, as literally millions of refugees, most of them Hindus, trekked into the packed camps organized by New Delhi.[11]

To make matters worse for India, both the U.S.S.R. and the United States appeared to be reducing their level of concern. In June, while Indian Foreign Minister Swaran Singh went looking for support in Moscow, Bonn, Paris, Ottawa, and Washington, Aleksei Kosygin paid a state visit to India to discuss this matter as well as other aspects of Indo-Soviet relations. The joint communiqué issued at the end of the meetings called for a political solution that would "answer the interests of the entire people of Pakistan."[12] As Professor Rushbrook-Williams notes, this was read in Islamabad as a Soviet move *away* from support for Bangladesh.[13]

The moderate tone of U.S. policy was, at least to India, belied by the secret trip of Dr. Henry Kissinger to Peking in July. Officially, Kissinger had gone to Islamabad to "talk with Yahya Khan," presumably about the crisis, after having gone to Delhi in the wake of Kosygin's discussions in India about an Indo-Soviet treaty of friendship, peace and cooperation. In fact, Kissinger's principal purpose in Islamabad was to secretly board a Pakistan International Airlines flight to Peking to discuss President Nixon's China visit. For both the Awami League shadow government and Mrs. Gandhi, the fact that Kissinger had chosen to go to China from Pakistan, and that he had decided to go to Peking at all, seemed to mean that the United States was wholly unlikely to support India in the subcontinent's growing troubles. The global priorities of U.S. policy were at this

---

[11] There are no precise figures on the number of refugees because of the inability to tell an East Bengali from a West Bengali, and because the very nature of the crisis forced governments to use statistics as part of their propaganda. The Pakistani government, in a particularly unconvincing way, said that there were exactly 2,002,623. In July, the Indians were equally precise and equally unconvincing, noting 6,733,019. The final Indian government estimates of 9 million were about 2 million higher than the autumn World Bank estimates, but all parties were clearly guessing. Suffice it to say that millions of people fled the violence who would not have left their land had not the risks of staying been incredibly high.

[12] It was this communiqué that informed Deshpande's view (in Ayoob et al., *Bangla Desh: The Struggle for Nationhood*) that the U.S.S.R. would probably not intervene in the crisis.

[13] Rushbrook-Williams, *The East Pakistan Tragedy*, p. 88.

time in maximum contradiction with regard to India and in maximum harmony with regard to Pakistan.

The Indian Dilemma

Thus, by July, the Indian government found itself in a difficult position. Its semi-open support for the Mukti Bahini guerrillas, for the government-in-exile, for a "radio Bangladesh" in Calcutta, and for the Awami League cause internationally had not brought Yahya Khan down, nor had it appreciably weakened the Pakistani army in East Pakistan, nor did it show any promise of doing so in the immediate future. Moreover, millions of refugees were on Indian soil, producing a grave financial crisis and ever more explosive political problems.[14]

There were two other factors of major importance in the Indian government's review of the problem. The first was the danger that the Awami League leadership would disintegrate and that the league would be transformed into either an all-Bengal regional nationalist movement,[15] or a guerrilla Communist movement increasingly dependent upon Chinese support,[16] or both. In Sisir Gupta's analysis,

> As the resistance movement grows and its base widens, it will inevitably acquire far more radical qualities than it now possesses. In fact, the radicalization of the resistance movement is a pre-condition of its successes. *If the struggle in Bangla Desh has to be waged on many fronts, it cannot be conducted by moderates alone.*[17]

---

[14] *The Economist*, 30 October 1971, put the matter vividly. The problem was twofold, "how to pay for them, and how to send them back whence they came." In the short term, international aid was necessary; yet total aid for India was falling. "The refugees have destroyed that prospect [for economic growth] like a swarm of locusts."

[15] Mrs. Gandhi's statements of support for the Awami League were very carefully limited to a defense of the autonomy of the people of East Bengal. "Bangladesh," the land of the Bengalis, had much wider connotations and was not used by the Indian government until December.

[16] During the crisis, the leader of a supposed pro-Peking party, Maulana Abdul Hamid Khan Bahashani, was, according to British press reports and his cousin's testimony, under house arrest in New Delhi. He returned to East Bengal (or was returned to Bangladesh) after the Awami League government was installed in Dacca.

[17] Ayoob et al., *Bangla Desh: The Struggle for Nationhood*, p. 172 (italics added). See also Ruth Glass, "Bengal Notes," *Monthly Review*, vol. 23, no. 5 (October 1971), pp. 17-42, for a discussion of the revolutionary potential of a united, left Bengal.

The other factor in New Delhi's calculations was the regional strategic balance in the subcontinent. Ever since 1954 and the beginning of American arms assistance, Pakistan had countered Indian actions and frustrated Indian efforts to play a wider role in world and regional politics. The placement of a large Pakistani army at the approaches to Kashmir forced India to immobilize a substantial part of its army in a static defensive posture. Moreover, Pakistan had consistently involved other great powers in the quarrels of the sub-continent, most recently and dangerously, China. The well-equipped Pakistani army of about 350,000 men was supported by a society of over 120 million and Pakistan's foreign exchange earnings were large. Without East Pakistan, the country would shrink to about 55 million, a little less than half of its foreign exchange earnings would be lost, and it could not afford to maintain such a large military establishment. It was a golden military opportunity for India to eliminate the Pakistani threat.[18]

It is also conceivable that New Delhi saw a possible "second phase" Mukti Bahini guerrilla movement as potentially successful, and as being remote from Indian influence. If the struggle had gone on, the Awami League émigrés in Calcutta and the pro-Indian Mukti Bahini (and Mujib Bahini) would have lost control of the struggle. A major Indian military effort would foreclose that possibility and build the basis for close India-Bangladesh cooperation. This seems to have been one of the considerations behind India's encouragement of the five main East Bengali political parties' formation of an eight-member consultative committee in Calcutta to advise the Bangladesh government-in-exile and "to provide closer ties to the Mukti Bahini." This committee formed on 9 September 1971.

While all of these calculations supported Indian intervention, there were also risks and costs in such an action. The great powers would not support it, and might apply sanctions to India. Further, it would be difficult to justify an armed invasion in support of an ethno-linguistic nationalist movement without seeming to justify similar action by others toward India's disgruntled minorities. The greatest peril lay in the war itself, which would certainly widen, and which might bog India down in the Ganges Delta for a generation. Even if India won a military victory, it might be "stuck" with a dependency that was both unstable and demanding, and whose independence might stimulate leftist movements in eastern India.

[18] This was essentially the argument of the much discussed K. Subramanyan paper, written from the Indian Institute for Defense Studies and Analysis in the fall of 1971. A more detailed statement in the same vein is in Ayoob and Subramanyan, *The Liberation War*.

India Prepares to Intervene

During the summer and early autumn, the Indian government began planning strategies to minimize each of these risks, while following a declaratory policy aimed at building pressure on Pakistan to deliver a political settlement. It was classic diplomacy at its best.

The first task was to get Soviet support for a direct Indian military intervention in Bangladesh. This would offset both the Chinese and the American roles—the Chinese by presenting them with a Soviet military "guarantee" in support of India, and the Americans by cancélling out such U.N. activity as Washington might attempt. On 9 August 1971 India and the U.S.S.R. announced the signing of a twenty-year Treaty of Peace, Friendship and Cooperation, and accompanied the announcement with news that Russia would provide India with more arms. The prospect of such a treaty had been under consideration since Leonid Brezhnev had mooted plans for an Asian collective security system in 1969. India had not accepted his idea, pleading "nonalignment." In the summer of 1971, however, events in the subcontinent made the treaty highly desirable, and India pursued the opportunity. It was in this context that the Indians publicly stated that "We would never have signed the treaty of friendship with the Soviet Union if Dr. Kissinger had not made it clear that India was outside the American defense system." When this was denied by American diplomats, the Indians insisted that he had said "India could be no part of the United States defense commitment." [19] The background for this statement is presumably the Kissinger summer consultation in New Delhi about which Jagdish Bhagwati, a careful observer, states, "In case of war with Pakistan, Kissinger is supposed to have said, China would come in and India would not get any American help as she had in the Sino-Indian War of 1962." [20] This was significant because India expected trouble with China over its Pakistani policy. In any case, the United States repeatedly made it clear that it would not support India in military action against Pakistan, and it was obvious that at a time when the President was attempting to normalize relations with Peking as part of his global diplomacy he would not as a matter of course follow policies irritating to China. Whatever the rationale, the benefits of the treaty were obvious to both India and the U.S.S.R.—India in the short term and the U.S.S.R. over the long run.

---

[19] *The Daily Telegraph* (London), 29 October 1971.
[20] *Daedalus*, vol. 101, no. 9 (Fall 1972), p. 33.

The second Indian task was to eliminate the problems involved in "foreign intervention" by dramatizing the fact that the frontiers between India and East Bengal were illusory. The flood of refugees made that fact increasingly obvious, and India's eloquent argument that it was being victimized by events over which it ought to have some reasonable control was generally accepted. Pakistan's weak reply that the Indians, by supporting the guerrillas and offering them arms and sanctuary, had made the problem immeasurably worse was barely heard except in Washington. Poor press coverage, the reports of widespread atrocities, the obvious sectional inequities of the Ayub Khan era, and the clumsy Pakistani handling of news and diplomacy all provided India with the high ground from which to dominate the international public debate. By late autumn, the Pakistani army had apparently "won" most of the main battles in East Bengal, but the Indians were winning increasing world support for Bangladesh and international aid for the refugees. A later United Nations General Assembly vote—104 to 11, with 10 abstentions— favoring an immediate cease-fire and withdrawal of forces, seemed to show that most countries did not think the Indian case justified military intervention. Yet, neither did they strongly condemn it nor effectively support an "illegitimate and brutal" suppression of Bangladesh by West Pakistan.

The third task before India in the summer was to plan an effective, "surgical," military operation that would limit the war and, more especially, limit the time that Indian troops were actually fighting in East Bengal. If India did not have prompt success in its campaign, two developments were almost sure: The first would be that the world would conclude that the government of Pakistan had more support in Bengal than had been supposed, and therefore that the Indians were aggressors rather than liberators. The second would be an increasing concern and involvement on the part of the global powers as the conflict escalated. The war had to be fought on the Israeli "quick-victory" model before "international peace-keeping" came to Pakistan's rescue.

Indian military planners had three operational problems to meet. The first was to deny the Pakistani forces operating in East Bengal the opportunity to group themselves in strong defensive positions protecting the major population and production centers. The only way to do this was to increase the level of Mukti Bahini action and make that action province-wide. The Pakistani army would then have to spread its forces and, given the difficulties of movement in the province, they would have extreme problems in reconcentrating at the moment of Indian attack. Moreover, if the campaign was to be brief, the invading Indian forces would need local support both for intelligence and for the protection of key transportation points during their invasion.

Throughout the late summer, Mukti Bahini tactics did change from pitched border battles to widespread terrorism and sabotage. Moreover, the types of weapons used against the Pakistani army increased in variety and size. The degree to which this was planned in India is in part revealed by the report that the Indian army trained an organization called the Mujib Bahini, an army 5,000 strong, at Dehra Dun (the Indian military academy in North India). A British journalist reported: "They were instructed to return to strategic areas in Bangla Desh and lie low until they could team up with the Indian army after the outbreak of hostilities. Mr. Bangali [the group leader] admitted that he knew when the war would break out." [21] The reporter's discussion with other members of the group made it "apparent that his organization is under the direct command of the Indian Army." [22]

The second military problem was to concentrate an effective strike force on the frontiers of East Pakistan, and to equip that force with transportation capabilities that would be effective in the Ganges Delta. On the western side of East Bengal, such a force was easy to move but quite visible to Pakistani military intelligence. In the north and east, it was difficult to position but much more secure.

The calendar was decisive for Indian military planners concerned with rapid advance. The monsoon rains end in late summer and the period of maximum danger from floods is August-September. The harvest generally occurs in October, and the dry season begins in November. The winter crop is planted in December for harvest in spring. November is, in short, the best month for battle, both climatically and economically. It was the month that allowed the Indians to exploit their superiority in the air and with armor. It was also the best month for the Pakistani army to exploit its superior arms against the Mukti Bahini and consolidate its control.

The third military problem to be faced was the probability of a major Pakistani strike from the west wing toward Kashmir at the onset of an Indian invasion in the East. This required the stiffening of defensive positions and garrisons in western India and Kashmir,

---

[21] Peter Hazelhurst, in *The Times* (London), 31 December 1971. There is also some evidence in Major-General D. K. Palit, *The Lightning Campaign* (Salisbury: Compton, 1972).

[22] *The Times* (London), 31 December 1971.

and a readying of Himalayan posts for a possible Chinese diversionary action. Any hope that the U.S.S.R. would mount diversionary attacks against the Chinese in Sinkiang, should they strike in the Himalayas, would not take the pressure off the Indian forces first attacked. It was therefore necessary to minimize the chances that the Chinese would come to Pakistan's assistance. This counseled delay until the coming of bad weather in the Himalayas in November. At that time, the Himalayan reserve could be transferred to the West Pakistan frontier to counter the expected attack. By late October, the Indian army was able to report to the cabinet that it was ready, that it could assure the government that East Bengal would become Bangladesh within eight weeks, and that it *must* move in November.

The Indian government considered the problem of Bangladesh dependency upon New Delhi, and the possible consequences of the war on both the strength of the left parties and on Bengali regionalism in Indian politics. These were problems that could not be easily managed, but that would deepen unless Bangladesh became independent immediately and unless Mujibur Rahman and the other moderate Awami League nationalists took power. Private Indian diplomacy encouraged the efforts of the U.S.S.R. and the West to warn Yahya Khan not to kill Mujibur Rahman on the treason charge that had been brought against him.[23]

In late October, Mrs. Gandhi undertook a "damage limitation" diplomatic tour to the capitals of the Aid-India Consortium of the World Bank.[24] The ostensible purpose of the trip was to apprise these governments of the burden placed on India by the 9 million Pakistani refugees. Mrs. Gandhi's position was clear: India had exercised great forbearance and had undergone great sacrifice while an oppressive tyranny had committed atrocities and had suppressed a genuine national movement. India was not in a position to bear these burdens any longer. Unless massive assistance for the refugees and for India was forthcoming, and unless it was coupled with a settlement in East Bengal that would lead to the refugees returning home, India would act militarily to create that settlement. It was, in plain terms, "put up or shut up."

---

[23] *U.S. Foreign Policy for the 1970's: The Emerging Structure of Peace*, A Report of President Richard Nixon to the Congress, 9 February 1972 (Washington: Government Printing Office, 1972), p. 145, notes: "We obtained assurance from President Yahya that Sheikh Mujibur Rahman would not be executed," but it gives no other details.

[24] In early November, the West Pakistani junta sent A. Z. Bhutto to Peking in an effort to offset the traveling Indian diplomacy.

In the late October Paris meetings of the World Bank, the donors agreed that the refugees were an "international responsibility" but there were no new major commitments.[25] And Delhi asked, was India supposed to *borrow* from the creditor nations to meet problems caused by events in Pakistan, when that same Pakistan had defaulted upon its loan repayments so that it could fight a civil war? This was an especially sensitive subject because, while no new pledges of aid had been forthcoming for Pakistan, past commitments were being honored in spite of debt default.[26]

In Bonn, Paris and London, governments were unwilling or unable to "put up" new aid efforts and public opinion as well as government opinion was clearly pushed toward a pro-Bangladesh/pro-Indian position. Pakistan was being progressively isolated. Most observers agreed with the articulate Bengali economist-in-exile, Rahman Sobhan, who argued that Bangladesh was inevitable; the question was only how soon and at what cost. India was promising prompt and inexpensive independence. At the end of her successful European tour de force Mrs. Gandhi arrived in Washington to a very cool reception.

Mrs. Gandhi would have done well to have reviewed the previous five years of American diplomacy. After the 1965 Indo-Pakistani War, the United States modified its South Asian posture and the magnitude of its commitments. It accommodated itself to a greater Soviet and Chinese presence, and defined these developments as acceptable to its global posture. American economic assistance continued to flow to both Pakistan and India in large quantities (see Table 1), but the level of intimacy in diplomatic, military and political contact was considerably reduced from the high points of the late 1950s and early 1960s. It seemed to a succession of U.S. administrations that South Asia was peripheral to American vital interests, economic and strategic, and that the area's essential claim on resources was humanitarian.

When the Ayub Khan regime fell and the dirty linen of corruption and developmental inequities became known publicly in the United States, U.S. aid administrators and planning officials revealed

---

[25] It was clear that only the United States was in a position to do so, and Indo-American relations had become tense.

[26] This was the principal bone of contention between India and the West, India arguing that all aid should be cut thus forcing Pakistan to its knees. The aid consortium argued that the destruction of the Pakistani economy would ensue, that the Indus River projects could not be aborted without irreversible damage, and that aid sanctions would hurt the people, not the regime, which could be pressured by other means.

Table 1

U.S. ECONOMIC GRANTS AND CREDITS TO INDIA AND PAKISTAN, 1947–1970
(in $ millions)

India		Pakistan	
Total, 1947–70	$8,228	Total, 1947–70	$3,438
1964	864	1964	377
1965	854	1965	349
1966	760	1966	220
1967	838	1967	331
1968	576	1968	278
1969	466	1969	209
1970	432	1970	239

Source: *U.S. Statistical Abstract, 1971* (Washington: Government Printing Office, 1971), p. 760.

a commitment to "distributive justice" and "federal balance" in Pakistan.[27] This paralleled President Yahya Khan's slightly biased (in favor of the East for a change) development budget that appropriated 53 percent of the investments for Bengal. In cooperation with the U.S. Agency for International Development and the World Bank consortium, special East Pakistan action projects were elevated to high priority status.

Yahya Khan's measured walk toward democracy had also been welcome in Washington because it reduced the criticisms that had been leveled at American aid to dictatorial regimes. In the process of adjusting the economy to take heed of Bengal's special claims, and in re-creating a parliamentary system in Pakistan, Yahya Khan was receptive to American advice, and his policies reflected this. In political terms, Washington and Islamabad grew closer together than they had been since the 1962 Sino-Indian War.

When the civil war rocked Pakistan, it also rocked relations between the U.S. and the Yahya Khan regime. As the refugee flow greatly increased, the tolerant U.S. stance toward Pakistan declined in the face of Indian criticism and the criticism of the public debate

[27] *The Fourth Five Year Plan, 1970-75* (Karachi: Planning Commission, Government of Pakistan, 1970), forecast this change. "The development strategy of the 1970s has to change fundamentally. While essentially protecting the growth rate already achieved, a greater regional and social balance is being attempted in its composition" (p. 12).

in the United States. The immediate U.S. reaction was to cut military assistance and put a "hold" on all new economic assistance projects. Previously contracted aid was allowed to continue, however, while the U.S. quietly exercised its influence in an attempt to facilitate a political settlement of the civil war. This was correctly seen as forbearance by Islamabad, and Yahya Khan managed both to "postpone" debt repayments and to sustain a winning army in East Bengal during the period of that forbearance. The U.S. was, regardless of Yahya's strategy, unwilling to take steps that could lead to national division or to the destruction of West Pakistan's economy. It was a status quo policy with no real goals, and no sense of accommodation to regional change.

By the summer of 1971, when the civil war seemed to be going Pakistan's way, the public outcry against the suppression of Bangladesh had diminished in the U.S. The belated Pakistani white paper on the crisis revealed that some Biharis had died in atrocities before the army had intervened, that the intervention was much less "atrocious" than had been thought (or at least that all sides had committed atrocities), and that the Indian role in both the insurgency and the refugee flood was more important than had been realized. Above all, it reminded the world that Mujibur Rahman had not campaigned for a separate state, but for a considerable amount of provincial autonomy, and that the government of Pakistan was willing to grant a measure of decentralization that few other governments would be willing to accept. Pakistan's news management and diplomacy also became more effective, largely by pointing to India's growing role.

The Yahya Khan government went out of its way to court the' U.S. administration. Dr. Kissinger's trip to Peking via Pakistan was handled with remarkable finesse and perfect security. Pakistan's government later used this unrelated event both domestically and internationally to project the view that the U.S. basically accepted its posture in the civil war. When the Indians and the Russians signed the August treaty, Pakistan argued that India was no longer nonaligned and that the U.S.S.R. was moving into South Asia on a new footing. Above all, Islamabad kept Washington well informed about Indian defense movements and the threat of war. This was a stall, but Yahya Khan and his advisers believed that time was on their side, and they had developed some useful new issues in the crisis.

By October, it was clear to Washington that war was imminent, and that the United States would have to carry the main burden of avoiding it, if it was to be avoided. In short, the U.S. had to drop a policy of "restraint" and develop a policy of action. Earlier in the summer, Washington had initiated low-key talks with Britain, France and the U.S.S.R. in an effort to develop a formula of aid, diplomatic pressure, and arms-supply restraint that would allow the crisis to be moderated while Yahya Khan made his peace with Mujibur Rahman (or vice versa). This was unsuccessful, in part because of skillful Indian diplomacy in Moscow and Russian unwillingness to compromise the new Indo-Soviet treaty relationship. This left the burden with reluctant American policy makers.[28]

Mrs. Gandhi and President Nixon Have a Talk

When Mrs. Gandhi arrived for her talks with President Nixon, he had already made great efforts to find room for refugee assistance in his shrinking and unpopular foreign aid budget.[29] He had increased pressure on Yahya Khan to come to a political settlement with Mujibur Rahman, and had won grudging acceptance of the proposal that a designee of Mujibur Rahman should open talks in Calcutta on the question of maximum autonomy for East Bengal. He also knew that Indian diplomacy had been directed toward a heightening of the military crisis, the division of Pakistan, and Soviet support for what would soon be a war.

The President presumably opened the conversations in a conciliatory tone, but from the vantage point of a country that had been generous in assisting Indian development. He could reasonably have argued that war would lead to massive destruction of investment throughout South Asia, that it would not appreciably change the realities of the inevitable emergence of Bangladesh, and that it would compromise his ability to obtain continued congressional approval for economic assistance to India, a country that then would have used force against another American aid recipient.[30] He could report

---

[28] As President Nixon's foreign policy report phrased it, "because of our ties with both countries, in 1971 we were the only great power in a position to try to provide a political alternative to a military solution." *U.S. Foreign Policy for the 1970's: The Emerging Structure of Peace*, p. 143.

[29] The United States had appropriated new funds, or transferred from existing accounts, more than $160 million by October 1971. More funds were sought in the foreign aid bill, and additional Food for Peace wheat shipments were planned. By the onset of hostilities, the United States had pledged $500 million in cash and commodities. Ibid., p. 144.

[30] "As early as August 11, Secretary Rogers told the Indian Ambassador that the Administration could not continue economic assistance to a nation that started a war." Ibid., p. 146.

progress on the political settlement within Pakistan and could promise the continued use of American influence in Islamabad to produce such a settlement over the winter, perhaps as early as mid-December. It was true, he might have said, that the solution would not be an immediately independent Bangladesh, but it would be a relatively free state within a confederal system and in due course, probably an independent state. The real issue, as he no doubt said, was how to avoid war.

Mrs. Gandhi's position was equally clear. The civil war had brought India immense problems that would not automatically melt away, and which, as had already been demonstrated, the world would expect India to bear. Even if a settlement could be negotiated, which she doubted, it would leave Pakistani troops in Bengal and armed *Razakars* in the villages. Under these circumstances, the refugees would refuse to return to East Bengal and India's difficulties would continue.

India had responded to American pleas for restraint for six months, during which time things had worsened. No Indian government could indefinitely restrain popular support for Bangladesh, especially in the face of an evermore hostile and belligerent West Pakistani policy toward India. And India, as she perhaps reminded the President, was a democracy and she was going into crucial provincial elections in March 1972. She was not at all sure that a brief armed "police action" would lead to any more devastation than was being produced in the civil war, and it would at least bring the costs of intransigence home to the West Pakistani army. Would the United States prefer a bankrupt India, a brutally colonized East Bengal, a heavily mortgaged mini-imperial West Pakistan, and a Communist-led guerrilla insurgency in Bengal? [31]

It appears from the documents subsequently printed by Jack Anderson that there was no agreement between the parties on these issues.[32] The President's key point appeared to be whether a settlement could be arranged rapidly, but Mrs. Gandhi was equally interested in the nature of that settlement.

The American position was that Mrs. Gandhi should have been willing, if only for reasons of obligation to America, to forestall armed invasion while the political negotiations with Yahya Khan and

[31] In essence, this was the argument of Professor Robert Dorfman in the House of Representatives, Committee on Foreign Affairs hearings on 11 and 25 May 1971. He calculated an "occupation force" cost of $2 million a day.

[32] Minutes of the Washington Special Action Group, taken by Captain Kay, USN, for the Joint Staff of the Joint Chiefs of Staff, classified secret-sensitive, various dates during the course of the Indo-Pakistani War of December 1971.

the Bangladesh leadership were arranged.[33] That view ran directly counter to the military exigencies in eastern India, as seen by the Indian army, and to the political interests of Mrs. Gandhi who was preparing for the March elections. Mrs. Gandhi might reasonably have asked for steps to be taken against Yahya Khan that had some prospect of accelerating the process. In particular, she might well have asked for a complete embargo on any assistance for the regime until a settlement was reached, and it must have been clear to her that the proclaimed embargo was in fact "leaking" considerably.

It is unclear whether Mrs. Gandhi left Washington having refused to accept the American position, or whether she conveyed the impression that she would return home to do her best, reserving judgment about the course of action she would pursue.[34] It is, however, quite clear that the U.S. administration did not cancel economic assistance then in the pipeline to Pakistan. The American presumption must have been that India would honor the U.S. position with a further delay of the initiation of war, during which a political settlement would probably emerge from Islamabad and Calcutta. This was presuming too much.

Several other factors appear to have entered the Nixon administration's deliberations. The first was the Soviet role in South Asia and the Indian Ocean and, more particularly, in the crisis. The other was the international demonstration effect that an Indian invasion would have. Of the two, the former was clearly more immediately important.

On 27 October the U.S.S.R. and India released a statement, under Article 9 of the Treaty of Peace, Friendship and Cooperation, that declared that both parties fully agreed that Pakistan was about to launch a war of aggression in the subcontinent.[35] This statement was issued as N. P. Firyubin, the Soviet deputy foreign minister, left India for Moscow, and on the eve of Mrs. Gandhi's visit to Washington. This move had the appearance—intentional or not—of a diplomatic *fait accompli* that Washington had to accept. Mrs. Gandhi had not come to ask for peace, but to tell the President of the United States what she had decided to do. The Soviet offset to any American action,

---

[33] *U.S. Foreign Policy for the 1970's: The Emerging Structure of Peace*, pp. 146-147, makes it quite explicit that Washington expected the $4.2 billion of aid given or loaned between 1965 and 1972 to weigh heavily on Mrs. Gandhi's actions.

[34] The line she took with the press in Washington was: "the refugee situation in Bengal is about to blow. . . . We just can't wait much longer." ABC press conference transcript, Secretary of State Rogers, 5 January 1972. The citation was in a question asked by Howard K. Smith.

[35] *The Times* (London), 28 October 1971.

whether in the U.N. or in the Indian Ocean, appeared to have been arranged. This ran counter to Washington's post-Tashkent view that U.S. and Russian policies were parallel in South Asia, and coupled with Indian troop placements and covert use, made Mrs. Gandhi's public statements hypocritical at best, insulting at worst.

This set of surmises about Washington's reaction to Indian policy is given a little circumstantial confirmation in an article by Peter Jay in the London *Times*.[36] Henry Kissinger is said to have told a visiting British statesman that "he regarded India's invasion of East Bengal in the same light as Hitler's reoccupation of the Rhineland." When the British visitor disagreed with this view, stressing the essentially local and perhaps justified nature of the Indian act, Kissinger is said to have asked his visitor whether he knew anything about U.S.-U.S.S.R. relations. The Europeans, he continued, had avoided provocative statements and played the winner's game. In so doing, they had allowed a Russian-guaranteed invasion to occur with only the U.S. protesting. If this was going to be the "virtue" of a Soviet treaty of peace, friendship and cooperation, the world would be in for some troubled days.[37]

While there was a recognition that the initiative in the subcontinent was Indian and that India was the major regional power, it was also clear that Soviet support was decisive in giving India the military confidence to move. Not only had the U.S.S.R. supplied India with $730 million worth of arms since 1965, but it had also offered a treaty which, "together with new arms deliveries and military consultations, gave India additional assurance of Soviet political support as the crisis mounted." [38] The Soviet "crime" was apparently "aiding and abetting"—not directly committing the offense, but using it to enhance its position in South Asia and the Indian Ocean.

---

[36] "History Repeats Itself for Mr. Kissinger," *The Times* (London), 31 December 1971. On the other hand, Clare Hollingsworth, writing in *The Daily Telegraph* (London) on 29 October 1971, reported that N. Firyubin had failed in his attempt to get Mrs. Gandhi to postpone her visit to the U.S. and Europe, but the reason is unclear. He also reports that "the Russians appear anxious to lessen the tension between India and Pakistan."

[37] *U.S. Foreign Policy for the 1970's: The Emerging Structure of Peace*, p. 150, is particularly outspoken on this problem: "For the United States to compete with the Soviet Union in fueling an arms race [$730 million arms sales to India, compared to $70 million U.S. sales to both India and Pakistan since 1965] obstructing U.N. efforts to stop a war, and threatening China, was out of the question."

[38] Ibid., p. 149.

The other aspect of American policy that occupied a large part of the official declarations concerned the precedent that would be set by intervening in a "nationalities" problem in a neighboring state.

> Internal ethnic conflicts and separatist strains, moreover, are a phenomenon of the contemporary world. India, *more than most*, has a heavy stake in the principle that such instability should not be exploited by other countries through subversion or resort to arms. The alternative is a formula for anarchy. The unanimity of third world countries against this war was testimony of the universality of this concern.[39]

Whether this point was made with as much vigor in Washington before the war as it was in the postmortem is unclear.

Whatever might have been the result of the Nixon-Gandhi talks, the actual outcome certainly was not agreement. War was in the wings, and in November it took center stage.

---

[39] Ibid., p. 149. (Italics added.)

4

THE INDO-PAKISTANI WAR AND THE BIRTH OF BANGLADESH

The war followed a predictable pattern.[1] Indian troops, with excellent intelligence on fortifications and transport facilities, moved into East Bengal, were greeted as liberators by the local population, imposed a full blockade on all ports, and took command of the air. Pakistan responded by launching an attack toward Kashmir interests, which though initially successful, weakened as it ran into very strong resistance. Pakistan kept a large percentage of its first-line aircraft in reserve, and had to maintain a strong defensive force in West Pakistan to meet the Indian strikes along the Sind and Punjab frontiers. It was a replay of the 1965 war, with the exception that East Pakistan was brought into the battle and taken by Indian forces.

General Niazi, army commander in the East, apparently had refused to put into operation a defensive realignment of forces on 9-10 November when an Indian attack became imminent.[2] This would have meant a retreat, the Mukti Bahini would have marched in, and the country would have been smaller for it. Instead, he kept his troops on the frontiers and in the garrison towns. Once the Indians had invaded, he did not order retreat and reconsolidation until 6 December, a day after the U.S.S.R. vetoed a Security Council

---

[1] The sole exception was the 3 December Pakistani air force attack on Indian airfields which provided India with a formal *casus belli*. Had Pakistan sought war, it could have used the loss of three F-86s to Indian air force fighters in East Pakistan on 22 November, or the Indian army incursion around Boyra in East Pakistan on 21 November, when thirteen Pakistani M-24 tanks were destroyed five miles within Pakistani territory on the grounds that they "threatened Indian defensive positions," as pretexts. Earlier large scale Indian army support for the Mukti Bahini was less visible, but equal "cause."

[2] This account is based on Clare Hollingsworth's account of the Commission of Inquiry established by President Bhutto after the defeat. *The Daily Telegraph* (London), 18 January 1972.

cease-fire resolution. On the 7th, the governor of East Pakistan, in panic, sent a cable: "Our losses very heavy. Front in both Eastern and Western Sectors has collapsed. Jessore had already fallen. No communications, thus administration ineffective. As food, other supplies running out, even Dacca City will be without food in seven days."[3] Most of the information in this dispatch was substantively incorrect, but a last line in the message seems to have caught the spirit of the West Pakistani forces in the East: "Is it worth sacrificing so much when end seems inevitable?"

After some confusion about the proper course of the war, and very rapid strides of Indian forces in leap-frogging the rivers protecting Dacca, General Niazi went to the U.S. consul-general and asked if U.S. military assistance was to be provided.[4] He was assured that it was not, and the surrender was then communicated, via a U.S. State Department cable via Washington, to New Delhi.

U.S. Response to Indian Intervention

Against the backdrop of these events, the United States appeared to be following a surprising course of action. In an outspoken "backgrounder," a government official later identified as Joseph Sisco, assistant secretary of state for Near East and South Asian affairs, vividly placed the blame for the war on New Delhi. A few days later, after a storm of protest within the United States about this policy statement, Henry Kissinger gave a press conference to argue the administration's case.

At the 7 December briefing, Kissinger said that the U.S. had been using its influence for a political settlement, and for that reason had not made statements on any side. The administration had made $245 million in refugee relief aid available to India and Pakistan. Dr. Kissinger said that when he was in India and Pakistan he had informed both governments of U.S. aims and means, and that the foreign secretaries of both countries had agreed with the U.S. role.

---

[3] Ibid.

[4] This was not solely wishful thinking. G. W. Choudhury, citing an unpublished article by former ambassador Benjamin Oehlert, quotes the latter as writing "under instructions from the White House and the Department of State, acknowledging positively and without equivocation that our formal agreement to assist Pakistan in the event of aggression, even with our own armies, was not limited to Communist countries but indeed specifically includes India." (Personal conversation, 1972.) Professor Choudhury's forthcoming book will amplify this point.

He reported that on 19 November, two days before the war broke out, Washington had informed the Indian ambassador that it "was prepared to discuss a precise timetable for establishing political autonomy for East Pakistan," and that at U.S. urging the government of Pakistan had agreed: (1) that relief supplies should be distributed by international agencies so that the central government in Islamabad could not take credit for them, (2) East Pakistan should be returned to civilian rule by the end of December, (3) Pakistan should extend amnesty to all refugees, (4) Pakistan should withdraw its troops from East Pakistani positions bordering on India, (5) the United States should establish contact with the Bangladesh movement, and (6) Pakistan should negotiate with followers of the imprisoned Mujibur Rahman. Dr. Kissinger announced that either he or Secretary of State Rogers had met with the Indian ambassador twenty-five times to facilitate a settlement, and had conveyed the view to the Indian government that the U.S. favored autonomy for East Pakistan.[5]

The public debate continued as it transpired that the United States had suspended all economic project assistance for India, and that a carrier task force, led by the nuclear-powered aircraft carrier USS *Enterprise*, was steaming toward the Bay of Bengal. The assertions by Dr. Kissinger that the U.S. appreciated India's democratic practices and thus greeted its decision to go to war with sadness and disappointment, did not seem to square with the strength of the actual steps being taken by the administration, even though they were justified as either humanitarian or, in the case of the USS *Enterprise*, as an evacuation force for Americans in East Pakistan.

The end of the war found Washington very divided. The United States had adopted a futile posture of condemning the side that would obviously win, and which a large part of the American public believed should win. It had cancelled aid to a country that American leaders had said was being helped for humanitarian-economic reasons, and it had dispatched a carrier attack group to the waters of the largest democratic country in the world, presumably to threaten it in support of a venal, bumbling, military dictatorship

---

[5] This is a summary of the press conference in the White House on 7 December 1971. It was this briefing that prompted Ambassador Kenneth Keating to cable from New Delhi: "I feel constrained to state that elements of this particular story do not coincide with my knowledge of the events of the past eight months," 8 December 1971, reprinted in the *New York Times*, 6 January 1972, from the Anderson collection of secret documents. *U.S. Foreign Policy for the 1970's: The Emerging Structure of Peace*, pp. 145-146, modestly admits that there was no assurance of success in the political talks under way, but "they could have been supported and facilitated" if India had shown the interest.

involved in suppressing the majority of its citizens. Small wonder that Nixon administration supporters were left in bafflement, and its critics in sheer anger. Too much of American policy prior to the crisis had been sub rosa, and there was little consensus within the administration about the key questions when they were faced. In part, it was a case of private, closely guarded diplomacy suddenly exploding in public [6] with much of the decisive information about the problem and policy unknown, even within the administration.

Under such conditions, and in an election year, it was perhaps inevitable that documents would start to "leak" into the public domain. During the first week of January, Jack Anderson's syndicated column began carrying comments from the Washington Special Action Group's (WSAG) minutes, and when Dr. Kissinger said that he was being quoted out of context, Anderson released the full text to show the contrary.

The documents themselves shed little new light on the crisis. They seem to show that the President was his own secretary of state in the South Asian crisis, and that the National Security Council and the WSAG were management, not a consultative or planning group. They were not originally constituted as such, and the strains and confusion produced in the process are clear from the documents. The President apparently knew what he wanted done, and WSAG and the Washington bureaucracy were to find ways to do it.

In fact, short of direct military intervention, which was logistically difficult and politically absurd, there was very little that the United States could do to stop India from its actions. A U.N. resolution, sure to be vetoed by the U.S.S.R., could indicate official displeasure. New AID projects could be stopped.[7] Private statements could be issued. But there was no way to favorably influence the course of major events in the subcontinent, and that presumably was the object of American policy. Mrs. Gandhi had won.

---

[6] In his foreign policy report, President Nixon argued, for example, that "during the week of December 6, we received convincing evidence that India was seriously contemplating the seizure of Pakistan-held portions of Kashmir and the destruction of Pakistan military forces in the West." But when the USS *Enterprise* was ordered to the Indian Ocean is left unanswered, and what evidence the government had concerning Indian intentions that might have provoked U.S. *military* action against India is not specified. *U.S. Foreign Policy for the 1970's: The Emerging Structure of Peace*, p. 147.

[7] More or less, that is. Washington found it as difficult to stop aid to India as it had been to stop aid to Pakistan, and for many of the same legal and economic reasons. In light of India's protests against arms to Pakistan, it is interesting that when the $87.6 million economic assistance cut was made, Washington also cancelled $11.5 million in military sales licenses to India which was about three times the amount then outstanding in licenses for Pakistan.

It was then argued that U.S. policy steps should be seen not in a local, but in a global, context, and that the sending of the *Enterprise* task force into the Indian Ocean was more a signal to the U.S.S.R. than support for Pakistan. After the fact, but not wholly convincingly, American officials said that the U.S. took such steps because they believed that India intended to destroy Pakistani forces in the West and conquer Azad Kashmir,[8] and that in bilateral talks with the Russians as well as unilaterally, they forestalled that possibility. The Indians denied that such a plan ever existed, and asserted that they were continually on the defensive in the West. U.S.-Soviet relations in the crisis remain difficult to establish but certainly seem decisive to the last moves in the war.

The administration consistently argued that the major reason it made representations against India was that it disagreed with New Delhi's use of military force to solve a political problem in Pakistan. Secretary of State Rogers, when questioned very closely about this on 5 January, said simply: "If every political problem that is created in the world justified the use of armed forces then there is no end to war."[9] As long as the U.S. was involved in Vietnam, however, such statements lacked full moral force, but they did summarize the view that India, after the summer of 1971, had made a restored Pakistan union impossible by military and diplomatic actions.

The Nixon administration also had to deal with the treaty commitments that it inherited. The WSAG minutes make it clear that Dr. Kissinger was aware of the commitment of the United States (cited in the unpublished Oehlert article above) to defend Pakistan in the case of aggression, even from India. Since that agreement was secret, and since the circumstances of the development of the war were so complex, it was impossible to develop a public diplomacy, other than the avoidance of war, that would serve the interests of both countries. And certainly the secret agreement allowed American passivity in the case of Pakistan's starting the war, as it clearly did in 1965. The honoring of agreements in international politics is a serious matter to a country with a large number of alliance partners, however, and part of the Nixon administration's reaction to the South Asia crisis may have developed from the preference for honoring such commitments, no matter how "flexible."

---

[8] Jack Anderson, in a *Playboy* interview (November 1972) noted that the paper concerning possible Indian redeployment and action against West Pakistan argued that it was *improbable*, but that this had been suppressed by the administration.

[9] American Broadcasting Company, 5 January 1972 press conference.

India Regionally Ascendant

The war ended on 17 December 1971 with the unconditional surrender of all Pakistani forces in East Bengal, and with a cease-fire along the western frontier from Sind to Kashmir. The West Pakistani military junta collapsed as General Yahya Khan surrendered the government to Z. A. Bhutto. President Bhutto's mandate was unclear, but he promptly arrested or dismissed Yahya Khan and seventeen other generals. As the "joint" India-Bangladesh forces were organizing 93,000 prisoners of war for transfer to Indian camps, Bhutto released his own principal captive, Sheikh Mujibur Rahman. Returning to Dacca via London and New Delhi, Mujib was briefed about the great tragedy that he had missed while in solitary confinement in the West. His proclamation of independence, however, had some of the fire of a dream realized. The old Pakistan was dead forever.

The West Pakistani population had been fed on managed news during most of the 1960s, and from the onset of the civil war in March 1971 they had been told of a series of victories. The December phase of the war left no one in doubt about the strength of Indian forces. Every major city in West Pakistan was attacked effectively by the Indian air force, and Karachi harbor was devastated by sea as the Indian navy savaged Pakistan's small fleet. The end of the war left so many prisoners in Indian hands that the magnitude of defeat could not be denied, and the weak performance of the army on the Kashmir front ended all talk of the superiority of the Muslim fighting man against his ancient Hindu foe. Mr. Bhutto's country was in shock—divided, bankrupt, and vanquished. The past fears of India, labeled paranoid by a disinterested world, had been "proven."

India emerged from the crisis as a newly purposive, powerful and skillfully managed regional power. Mrs. Gandhi's decisive policies won her near-universal praise in her own country and respect—even if it was grudgingly given—in Washington, Peking, and Moscow. The Indian armed forces proved to their countrymen and interested neighbors that they had recovered from the shameful performance of 1962 along the Sino-Indian frontier, and that they were capable of coordinated political-military action. Indian diplomats could feel with justification that their country's foreign policy was again dynamic after the post-Nehru recession. While some credit for the Indian success was owed to Moscow, most close observers realized that the Soviets had followed, not led, the Indians, and that whatever status the Russians had attained in the subcontinent was a consequence of Indian policy.

Bangladesh was upon creation a ravaged society of economic disorder and massive social dislocation in a region of historical poverty. Its people had borne a number of natural and human catastrophes within one generation: the great famine of 1943; the agonies of a partitioned Bengal in 1947; the burdens of poor refugees received and rich émigrés lost; painfully low production facing unparalleled rates of population growth; a decade and a half of exclusion from the decision-making centers of their own country; recurrent floods and cyclones; and the final insane anguish of assassination, rape, and destruction visited upon them by their "countrymen." The real power of the Awami League was the promise of self-rule that by itself would partially compensate for the misery inflicted by nature. Bangladesh might have been an economic wreck on the first day of its independence, but it was psychologically buoyant.

American relations with the three countries of South Asia after the war were understandably bad. Pakistan's leaders and public believed that they had been doubly betrayed by Washington; first, in the U.S. encouragement of Bengali separatists and, second, by failing to come to Pakistan's aid (in violation of security commitments) when it was attacked by India. The new president of the country was a self-confessed anti-American who had led a mission to Peking on the eve of the war. If issues were needed on which to break relations, they were present aplenty, and the public would have supported any such policy with enthusiasm.

Almost as a surrogate for its anger with the U.S., Pakistan left the Commonwealth and denounced Britain's recognition of Bangladesh. But the frustrating truth of the situation was that Mr. Bhutto's Pakistan needed the United States for the restoration of the economy, for its continued growth, and for military assistance if only in the form of spare parts for the large proportion of American equipment in the Pakistani military. The postwar revelations of the Nixon administration's "tilt" for Pakistan made it easier for Pakistan's new government to advance this policy to a skeptical country, and within a few months U.S.-Pakistan relations could be described as almost cordial, at least at the official level.

Relations with the new regime in Dacca were also bad. The East Bengal that the United States had begun to assist with new economic aid priorities in 1969 had, two years later, become independent in the face of American policy that appeared to be hostile to its emergence. Its leaders may have accepted the Washington view that it was "antiwar but not anti-Bangladesh," but the public was unconvinced. The Awami League's champions in the American consulate-general in Dacca had been reassigned early in the crisis, and the American embassy in Islamabad appeared to be counseling forbearance and patience with the Yahya Khan regime in spite of atrocities in the East. At best, American policy appeared to be biased in favor of sacrificing the secessionists—if not the "confederalists"— to the same fate as Biafra. The secessionists had taken power, however, and they remained suspicious of a Washington that delayed recognition in deference to Islamabad's sensitivities.

Like Mr. Bhutto, Sheikh Mujibur Rahman would probably have preferred to castigate the United States but could not because of Bangladesh's great need for economic and rehabilitation assistance. Bangladesh's leaders may have concluded that the Nixon administration was, for whatever reason, pro-Pakistan but that the U.S. Senate and public opinion was on their side. American assistance was almost universally perceived as "guilt money" by which the U.S. administration was attempting to atone for its callousness in the civil war, and by which the Senate could indicate its overall support for the new state. As in Pakistan, official relations between Bangladesh and the U.S. were better than public opinion would have justified, even before recognition in April 1972.

Indo-American relations were at the lowest ebb since Indian independence in 1947. If the disagreements between the two regimes before and during the war had not been divisive enough, the handling of the aftermath of the crisis alone would have caused severe problems. The "Anderson Papers" leak embarrassed Washington, provided New Delhi with new grounds for feeling aggrieved, and compromised the American ambassador in New Delhi by revealing that he was neither privy to, nor influential in, decisions relating to Indo-American relations during the crisis. The General Accounting Office report, released later, which showed that the magnitude of American arms supplies to Pakistan was considerably greater than previously reported gave yet another evidence of apparent bad faith.[10] Almost all of these "facts" were known to the Indian government during the crisis; the revelations contributed nothing new to Indo-American relations except a public bad odor.

Leaving aside the substantive problems of Indo-American relations, which would have made this crisis extremely difficult to manage in any case, the main difficulty stemmed from the sudden public disclosure of aspects of a private diplomacy. U.S. policy was in part

---

[10] Tad Szulc, writing in the New York Times of 22 June 1971, concluded that U.S. sales to the Pakistani air force alone between 1967 and 1970 were almost $48 million, much more than was ever publicly announced.

one of reaction to Soviet and Chinese postures, with both Peking and Moscow dealing with the Bangladesh crisis in terms of their global objectives. The Indian take-over of the insurgency in mid-summer had been little noted, and the private American diplomacy of seeking Indian restraint in the war fell afoul of Sino-American and Indo-Russian developments in July and August. The Pakistan-Bangladesh crisis was an embarrassment to every great power and an enormous liability to India, the more so because of the remarkably inept government in Islamabad. Very few elements of this situation "showed" and the Nixon administration attempted to avoid involvement, or the show of involvement, as long as possible. India, concerned with resolving the crisis quickly, had to follow an exactly opposite course and could make its position almost wholly visible as part of its diplomacy. No policy can be judged by what might have been, but after the fact many observers would conclude that a "confederal Pakistan" without an Indo-Pakistani War would have been infinitely preferable to the actual outcome. Few Indian decision makers, however, shared that view at the time. This difference of perception and of interest was what lay between Americans and Indians in the winter of 1971.

Once done, however, the negative American policy toward India coupled with press revelations posed new problems in restoring a modicum of civility in relations. India's position, while militarily strong, was not unlike that of Pakistan and Bangladesh in regard to concern for American economic support and assistance. The war was hard on Indian foreign exchange holdings and on domestic price stability.[11] India's generous aid to Bangladesh came from a temporary grain surplus that was completely eroded in the bad 1972 monsoon season, and in 1973 India had to import, at foreign exchange cost, food grains to avoid localized famine.

Two years after the event, Mrs. Gandhi's diplomatic-military finesse appears an almost hollow gesture purchased at the expense of real Indian priorities for stable development. Yet India's continuing need for American economic assistance and America's continuing advantage in reasonably good relations with New Delhi must overcome a bitter legacy. And unlike Sheikh Mujibur Rahman and

---

[11] The Indo-Pakistani War and the suspension of U.S. economic assistance left India in 1971 with a balance-of-payments deficit of $540 million, $290 million above projected levels. The debt service in 1972 was $600 million and Aid-India Consortium aid with U.S. contributions was at a level of $900 million, barely balancing trade and debt service deficits. *The Economist*, 29 January 1972.

Z. A. Bhutto, Mrs. Gandhi is not so dependent upon the United States that she must swallow her pride in order for India to survive. War's end, therefore, left India and America estranged, and many of the factors that contributed to the estrangement remain.

India-Pakistan-Bangladesh Relations

The government of India made it clear that its victory in the field would be followed by a diplomacy that would reorganize relations between the three principal countries of the subcontinent. While noting that it would do nothing to violate the independence of Bangladesh or the territorial integrity of West Pakistan, it would insist that regional relationships be entirely devoid of third-party interference. This position is a historic one aimed at restoring the Indian hegemony that existed until the Pakistani-American arms agreement of 1953-54.

In the first phase of postwar diplomacy, Mrs. Gandhi's public statements were uncompromising. She argued that all Pakistan-Bangladesh issues involved in the division of the state were to be settled bilaterally between Dacca and Islamabad, and that India would not conclude its peace talks with Pakistan until there was Pakistani recognition of the reality of Bangladesh.[12]

India also insisted upon a "straightening" of the Kashmir cease-fire line in its advantage, and upon an agreement converting the cease-fire line in Kashmir to a de facto, mutually accepted, international frontier. If these conditions were met, India would withdraw from Pakistani territory, repatriate POWs and normalize other aspects of relations.

These demands were made upon an extremely weak Pakistani government, one in which Mr. Bhutto was still attempting to consolidate his control while reassuring the shocked country of its own future. An added irony of the situation was that Mr. Bhutto was perhaps the most anti-Indian politician in Pakistan's public life. From the 1965 Tashkent agreement until the civil war he had monotonously vilified India, much to his political success. The Pakistan People's party, led by Bhutto, had attained its strongest positions in the districts bordering India where security fears are the greatest, and his influence with younger army officers appears to

---

[12] In a policy reversal, Mrs. Gandhi said in February 1972 that India would not make Bangladesh recognition a prerequisite to Indo-Pakistani peace talks.

have been considerable. In sum, Mr. Bhutto's domestic position did not allow him to accept the Indian demands, while his international position gave him no choice but to accept them. In this dilemma, Bhutto did the only things he could do—he stalled and uttered ambiguous, self-contradictory, statements.[13] This proved an excellent posture, both internally (where a pliant press reported Pakistan's strength) and externally (where Mrs. Gandhi found that she could not bring him to the table by force).

The second phase of India-Pakistan-Bangladesh relations was initiated at the July 1972 Simla conference. In this period the Indian government adopted a conciliatory position which, in fact, separated the India-Pakistan issues (the western front and Kashmir) from the Pakistan-Bangladesh issues. India wanted the status quo ante along the western front except in Kashmir, where it wanted some favorable modification of the cease-fire line and a Pakistani agreement to end the evocation of external powers in the Kashmir dispute. Under this formula, de facto Indian control might be questioned by Pakistan, but it would agree not to seek international support for its position. The United Nations force in Kashmir could thus retire, and Indian control be assured without Mr. Bhutto having to explicitly sign away part of the Pakistani dream.

The other issues discussed at Simla concerned the prisoners of war, whom India stated were under the joint control of Bangladesh and India, and hence would require Pakistan-Bangladesh negotiation if they were to be returned. Other related issues included the repatriation of Bengalis interned in Pakistan, and the problem of Urdu-speaking residents of Bangladesh who sought to emigrate to Pakistan. Mr. Bhutto personally accepted the reality of Bangladesh but noted that, as a democratic leader, he could not extend recognition without a national consensus.

It must have been clear after Simla that Pakistan's negotiating position was not as weak as had been supposed as long as Mr. Bhutto did not provoke India. Moreover, Mrs. Gandhi and Mr. Bhutto had impressed one another, or so it would appear, and Mr. Bhutto's greatest strength—his ability to resign and leave India once more to face the generals—was conspicuously paraded. By this time, both

---

[13] *The Times* (London) of 27 March 1972 reports Mr. Bhutto announcing the end of his policy of "confrontation" on Kashmir and a willingness to negotiate with India about its future, but also a conviction that he would resign before accepting a humiliating, blackmailed settlement to India's advantage. Little more than a year later, in asking for renewed arms assistance, he told a reporter that "We are still in a position to be India's equal." *Newsweek*, 16 July 1973.

parties were conducting a diplomacy of détente, and for it to be successful they had to separate Bangladesh from other aspects of their relations.

Agreement at Simla paved the way for the withdrawal of Indian forces, the return of territory, and an improved Indian position in Kashmir. More explicit Pakistani concessions were not necessary in light of India's de facto military position and the dismemberment of Pakistan. Moreover, India still held the "high ground" through the POW and air transit rights (over Indian territory) issues, and by virtue of superior economic and trade prospects. It was "half" an agreement, but it allowed Mr. Bhutto to continue to temporize, build domestic support for an accommodation concerning Bangladesh, and restore some measure of public confidence. It provided India with a demonstration of its regional status and signalled the promise of a more pliant Pakistan in the future.

The third phase of India-Pakistan-Bangladesh relations began with the efforts to resolve those inconclusive aspects of the Simla accord that dealt with Bangladesh. There are many complex issues in Pakistan-Bangladesh relations: disposition of economic assets (such as the stock of Pakistan International Airlines and Shipping Corporation) and liabilities (bilateral and World Bank development assistance loans), interned personnel (Bengali civil servants and soldiers in West Pakistan, Biharis in Bangladesh), the Pakistani POWs (held by India for a fictional India-Bangladesh high command), alleged war criminals (West Pakistani soldiers indicted for crimes against humanity and East Bengali civil servants and soldiers who might be tried for treason by Pakistan), trade and currency assets, evacuee property claims, and compensation to Bangladesh for Pakistani destruction during the civil war. India held the POWs to improve Bangladesh's bargaining position with Pakistan, and Pakistan stalled on significant negotiations while world opinion developed against India's clear violation of the 1949 Geneva POW accords.

In April 1973 the governments of India and Bangladesh put forward a proposal to resolve certain issues. India would return the Pakistani POWs, Pakistan would repatriate the interned Bengalis, and Bangladesh would send to Pakistan the more than 200,000 Urdu-speaking Biharis who had opted for citizenship in Pakistan. Bangladesh would maintain the right to bring almost 200 Pakistani officers and enlisted men to trial for war crimes. Pakistan's response to this proposal was mixed. A tentative affirmative was given to the prisoner exchange but was accompanied by a denunciation of the proposed trials and a threat to put on trial for treason Bengalis held in Pakistan. India sought by this proposal a disengagement from the Pakistan-Bangladesh relationship, forfeiting its distasteful hostages before more world attention was focused on New Delhi. This would leave a host of issues—from recognition through economics—to be settled bilaterally between Pakistan and Bangladesh (and, of course, the donor countries interested in debt repayment).

In each phase of negotiations, Mr. Bhutto's strength grew, both because his domestic strength was being consolidated and because the Indians were left with fewer and fewer bargaining levers. Whatever the justice of the case, Bangladesh was clearly the weakest party in the subcontinent, and its position one of great vulnerability.

Other reasons for Mr. Bhutto's relative success have been Pakistan's diplomacy, and especially continued American support in both economic assistance and, in the spring of 1973, military sales. Russia has been unable to further its position with India. Indeed, some Indians appear to have been alarmed at the notion of increasing dependence on the U.S.S.R.[14] China's position is even more weak. Its proffered trade deal with Bangladesh of March 1972 was turned down, and its resources are too limited to justify the risks of further alarming India. The Chinese veto of Bangladesh membership in the United Nations has further reduced the flexibility of Chinese diplomacy.[15] While the position of India is guaranteed by its size and domestic strength, and that of Pakistan, to a lesser extent, by its diplomacy and domestic potential, Bangladesh continues to play from a weak hand in regard to both the global and the regional powers. Sheikh Mujibur Rahman's visit to Moscow in March 1972 was to have yielded "the major share of a $3,000 million reconstruction programme."[16] It did not. The Chinese offer of trade without recognition was spurned. Indian assistance, very generous in the first year of Bangladesh independence, was an inherently limited case of the poor helping the poor. Western assistance to Bangladesh has been on a large scale, but "humanitarian" rather than developmental. As the chief of the Bangladesh Planning Commission said, perhaps more to make the point than to argue it, "The West won't let us starve, but it won't help us really develop."[17]

---

[14] *The Daily Telegraph* (London) reported that "Moscow pressure worries India's Defense Chiefs" as early as October 1971, and there is no evidence that Indo-Soviet military collaboration increased after the December 1971 war.

[15] 12 August 1972. It was the first veto cast by China after its admission to the United Nations.

[16] *The Times* (London), 2 March 1972.

[17] Interview with author, Dacca, October 1972.

U.S. Policy and "Normalization" in South Asia

The end of the Indo-Pakistani War left official Washington angry, embarrassed, and convinced of the hopelessness of attempting to play a constructive role in South Asia. American policy following hostilities was to do little and spend even less. Ambassadorial incumbents left Pakistan and India and were not replaced, and aid programs were either frozen or operated on the basis of momentum.

Ideally the United States might have undertaken an "agonizing reappraisal" and pursued one of a number of grand policy alternatives in South Asia: remaining distant from its central problems and dynamics, involving itself decisively with India in the management of regional problems of development and security, or rescuing Pakistan and continuing to play a moderately interventionist role in the crises of the subcontinent, if only to foreclose Soviet and Chinese monopolies.

In fact, almost immediately after the war the United States constructed a series of "small policies" designed to bring vital humanitarian assistance to Bangladesh, and within five months thereafter to recognize it as an independent state. This policy had nothing to do with overall subcontinental aims, and was not part of a coordinated strategy of producing some sort of balance in the region. It was, rather, a first step toward an accommodation to the new situation. An American consul-general remained in Bangladesh after its independence and, while lacking any formal credentials, was given almost every diplomatic prerogative. The elevation of the consulate-general to an embassy was merely an adjustment. Bangladesh's needs were pressing, and it was argued that diplomatic niceties were less important than getting a $200 million relief and reconstruction program moving. The policy on Bangladesh, therefore, was "humanitarianism."

Almost as promptly, the United States resumed economic assistance to Pakistan. From July 1972 to April 1973, the United States and the Aid-Pakistan Consortium delivered more than $340 million in assistance to the Pakistani government in commodity aid, on-going Indus River projects, and program loans. The economy responded to this stimulus with an export performance better than that of 1970 for the *entire* country, bringing into question for many Pakistanis the ideas of "exploitation" and efficiency that had previously been in vogue in explaining East-West relations. This assistance eased Mr. Bhutto's political-economic problems (all under his declared mantle of socialism) and was seen as a "rescue" operation to preserve the investments of the past in a viable economy. There was no intention of re-entering the subcontinent's regional problems, but rather simply allaying the dislocation problems of the Pakistani economy.

This was done even though military expenditures in Pakistan went up rather than down (and in March 1973 American arms-sales embargoes for the subcontinent were dropped). This policy benefits Pakistan more than India, but only a partisan could suggest that there is something ignoble about American arms sales and something acceptable about those of Russia, China, France, and Britain.

American "normalization" with India would also have proceeded apace but for Mrs. Gandhi's frequent sallies, which were returned in the same self-righteous tone in which they were delivered. The $87 million of prewar economic assistance that had been authorized but not delivered was "on again, off again" as recurrent irritations developed in Indo-American relations. It was a curious dialogue, with India publicly *haute* and aggrieved but privately accommodating, while the United States, publicly friendly and concerned for better relations, followed a private course of impatience. With U.S. assistance much reduced and U.S. military sales practically negligible, the Indo-American relationship cried out for reconstitution. It was not until the appointment of Professor Daniel Moynihan as ambassador to India (with still no word on appointments to Bangladesh and Pakistan) that the tone began to change. However, "normal" relations with India in the 1970s may well be a continuation of the carping, grumbling, and irritating relationship that emerged in 1971. Few considerations impel Delhi and Washington together; many issues lie between them, but most important, India's relevance to key American problems seems to be increasingly remote. "Benign neglect" may characterize a new set of Ambassador Moynihan's concerns.

In sum, the events of 1971 in the subcontinent led to less dramatic changes, both internally and externally, than was first thought. American influence seems the same as it ever was in Pakistan and Bangladesh, and the grumbling Indo-American relationship has become less important following the betterment of American relations with China and the U.S.S.R. The U.S.S.R. in the subcontinent must concern itself with both Chinese competition and Indian nationalism, and Moscow is not yet favored with bases or facilities in the region with which to extend its military influence. China is less significant in the region than before the 1971 crisis, and, perhaps, is also less interested in the region because of important changes in the strategic environment in northeast Asia and with the superpowers. While Pakistan remains friendly to Peking just as India remains friendly to Moscow, it is the same friendship of interest, not sympathy.

The division of Pakistan at first appeared to have broken the state's military strength. But because the army was entirely recruited from the western wing, and because the economy of the West may be stronger without the eastern wing, Pakistan's actual strength may not be much reduced. It is the great increase in India's forces which made the difference in the war, but armed forces are an expensive burden on both India and Pakistan.

India's regional ascendancy, therefore, is perhaps less marked than it appeared in 1971. The main security problem for India remains relations with China—in which the Indo-Soviet relationship remains a problem as well as an asset. Economic development needs make the West much more significant than the U.S.S.R. Population growth, inflation, social disorder, and economic inefficiency remain India's real enemies, and they cannot be banished by arms.

Bangladesh must remain on the conscience of the world. Its torment has been severe, and its claims on the rich world are compelling. Its self-government offers the opportunity for a humane, if not a rich or powerful, future for 75 million people. No Asian country has as many problems and as few assets with which to meet them as Bangladesh, however, and it is clear that this unfavorable social ratio is likely to produce turbulence and difficulties that will echo in eastern India. Bangladesh's leaders must know that to be ignored and abandoned is to be defeated, and their diplomacy will have to be highly active. This will introduce a dynamic factor into one of the world's most miserable but hitherto relatively quiet zones. For humanitarian and for strategic reasons, the United States will probably continue to have to have a regional diplomacy for Bangladesh, Burma and (eastern) India. The question is: What policy in what context?

5

AMERICAN POLICIES FOR THE SOUTH ASIA OF THE 1970s

It is highly unlikely that American foreign policy decision makers in the 1970s will concern themselves with the South Asian states on the same basis or with the same urgency as their predecessors in the late 1950s and 1960s. There have been important regional changes that have tended to strengthen nationalist regimes against both internal and external Communist influence. The regional balance of power is firmly established with India's hegemony evident. The U.S.S.R.'s regional role has been to strengthen India's position, both regionally and internationally. The only "unsatisfied" external power active in southern Asia is China, and it is increasingly clear that Chinese decision makers assign a relatively low value to interests in Pakistan. These conditions accord with American interests, in the main, and represent a strategic environment conducive to American military disengagement. South Asia is now a zone of peace, free of nuclear weapons and free of the direct presence of any of the great powers.

U.S. global strategy favoring lowered levels of competition with Communist adversaries has brought with it a measure of global normalization between those countries and the non-Communist world. The Sino-American détente, coupled with the end of the Vietnam War, establishes conditions in which the U.S. role can successfully be redefined in more modest terms. Under present technological conditions, the nuclear stalemate should begin to effect changes in Sino-Soviet relations that would reduce the main cause of tension in Asia in the early 1970s. Similarly, the Nixon-Brezhnev communiqués hold the promise of "restraint" in "third area" conflicts so that the "third world" might be defused as successfully as the "Two Germanies-Berlin" problem.

While these changes in regional and international situations have necessarily produced shifts in American foreign policy, a more potent influence has been the American domestic experience. The interventionist era in U.S. foreign policy, in which Washington assumed responsibility for worldwide military and economic management, oversaw decolonization and the development of a post-European world, and transformed itself into the world's first truly global power, has come to an end. The economic success of Europe and Japan, increasingly powerful Communist adversaries, and the groaning poverty and problems of Afro-Asian neighbors have changed the scale against which America measures its resources and power. The distasteful lesson in humility that these circumstances produced was exaggerated by the Vietnam War and its appalling political, personal, financial, and moral costs. With the harsh truth about the limits of power clearly seen, American decision makers in the 1970s must adjust goals and commitments to the fact of a more evenly balanced world distribution of wealth, influence, and the ownership of the means of violence.

The economic, diplomatic-political, and military assistance programs developed by the United States in the cold war period rested on the enormous and unique American resource base and the American political will to use national resources for international purposes. The transformation of the American economy from manufacturing to services and the growth of world demand has eroded the "free resources" once available to Washington while the U.S. view of itself and its future is one of resource scarcity.

As other societies have begun to reach levels of consumption per capita similar to that in the United States during the 1950s, real shortages of materials have begun to develop and price levels have risen. To the deprivation of the world's poor states, produced by their meager resource base and low level of capital investment, are now added higher import costs. Only those favored with large raw materials deposits—which the South Asian states are not—are relatively free of the threat of worldwide competition for the materials they need for their own development.

The diffusion of economic power that weakens the American ability to continue to play a dominant role in concessional resource transfers abroad, and establishes the national competition for resources that is becoming more intense, also means that the South Asian states cannot turn to any one national authority or one set of policy concerns in order to meet their national development needs. Indeed, the danger is that international assistance has lost a focal point, both in national terms and in ideological justification.

American resources will increasingly have to be used to protect and advance vital interests. A volunteer army, one of the "costs" of the Vietnam War, will be extremely expensive, as will the next generation of strategic weapons by which the central U.S.-U.S.S.R. military balance is maintained. The minimum "cover" for commitments in Korea, Western Europe and the Middle East will demand a larger share of a reduced American military budget.

U.S. exports must meet the costs of increasingly heavy energy imports and the products and services which Americans have come to expect from the world. They must also provide a stable base on which American firms can rely if they are to continue their overseas acquisition strategies. In this field, American agricultural products must play an important role and will henceforth be much less available for "free" transfer to developing countries with significant food shortages like India, Pakistan and Bangladesh.

Finally, the American will to use resources for international purposes has been greatly weakened by several contradictory developments. The new gestures of rapprochement with the Communist countries weaken the cold war rationale for global competition at the same time as a critical New Left charges that American assistance in the past has propped up reactionary regimes abroad. Americans have been somewhat disillusioned by the failure of past aid to solve major problems, by the absence of recipient respect for American policy (for example, the cases of India in 1971 and Pakistan in 1965), and perhaps most significantly by the impression that foreign aid is neither effective nor "honorable." Domestic demands on public resources are increasing in the United States, and almost all federal overseas projects are under siege from claimants within American society.

Under these conditions, a realistic American South Asia policy must accommodate the facts of a much reduced strategic commitment, fewer military resources available for transfer or regional contingencies, and a much reduced economic assistance program. The transition from a policy of profligate generosity to one of parsimony requires very careful consideration of specific objectives and specific problems. This sort of approach has not been a strong point of U.S. foreign policy since 1945, and it will require a major effort.

India

India is clearly the most important country in the region, both in national terms and in terms of its regional capabilities. Of all of the underdeveloped countries, India is perhaps the best endowed with resources, capital, infrastructure, and trained manpower. Its population and continental scale are both assets and liabilities, but, on balance, they offer the prospect of a development pattern that is basically autonomous.

There is no prospect for a "rich" India in the 1970s or 1980s or even, perhaps, in the twentieth century. The country is plagued by the kinds of problems and tensions which could shake its central institutions and produce domestic turbulence on a very wide scale. Development for India requires the creation of management institutions and economic productivity capable of providing a marginally better existence to a rapidly growing population and having enough surplus to sustain a defense force, an advanced science and technology, and an increasingly egalitarian social life.

American policy should be directed toward advancing India's capabilities in self-management and relatively independent economic and social development. It should also seek to ensure that no single great power is able to build a position of dominant influence in New Delhi.

Increases in Indian defense strength, especially in defense industry, are compatible with these goals. (India probably has the capability of building its military power to near equivalence with China if its leaders forsake other objectives.) India threatens no non-South Asian country with its present or projected strength, and it has no serious revisionist goals that would entangle it in war with either China or the U.S.S.R. It is not against American interests that Indian hegemony in the subcontinent should constitute a constraint for Pakistan's foreign policy managers, and the events of 1965 and 1971 must surely have convinced Islamabad that strategic accommodation is a more rational and desirable policy than an unstable, unreliable, and illusory balance of power based on fickle and distant external "balancers."

India's historic foreign policy has been more introspective than expansionist, and while it is possible that New Delhi will continue to mobilize resources for modest growth and self-management, it is most unlikely that there will be an export surplus available to power an "imperial India."

In all likelihood, the major problems of the international system in the 1970s will be nonmilitary problems produced by greater interdependence, the global security paralysis of strategic nuclear stalemate, and economic rivalry. In this kind of world, India's voice will be weak and its problems great.

Therefore, the United States should minimize its concern with India's military force developments, either in a positive or negative sense. Expansion of Indian defense industries will reduce Indian reliance upon Soviet arms assistance, but the world of the 1970s is likely to have many arms dealers and India will probably be able to purchase what it wants from any number of sources. These should include the United States.

Economic policies are likely to be much more important to India's future than those concerning arms, whereas in the past the situation was precisely the reverse. Assuming that some amount of economic assistance is available, the following steps might usefully be taken:

1. The United States should continue in its efforts to persuade Japan and the other Asian states to admit India, Pakistan and Bangladesh into the Asian Development Bank and the Japanese aid program.

2. The United States should continue to stimulate support for the World Bank Aid-India Consortium regardless of the decreasing annual U.S. contributions, perhaps by pointing to the past U.S. contributions.

3. The United States should reduce New Delhi's debt burden, accumulated over the past decade and now borne by Indian exports, by forgiving some debt and rescheduling much of the remainder under easier terms. This would represent "new aid" without the necessity for additional appropriations and would allow one of the most difficult Indian foreign exchange problems to be reduced.

4. The United States should insist, in concert with the European Common Market and world monetary managers, that less-developed countries be given preferential trade arrangements with all developed countries, and that Special Drawing Rights be integrated into multilateral aid commitments by the wealthier countries.

5. The United States should consider creation of a publicly funded bank that would acquire American-owned mining and manufacturing enterprises for resale to Indian private and public authorities. This would allow India to bring important elements of its economy under national control at no expense to American investors —whose capital, in any case, stands hostage to national confiscation or unprofitable regulated operation.

6. The United States should reduce the scale of its informational programs and increase assistance for Indian institutions and local educational and cultural processes. The emigration of highly trained manpower to the U.S. should be discouraged by changes in immigration and visa regulations in consultation with the Indian government.

7. The numbers of Americans in official and business positions in India should be reduced to avoid the "neo-colonial" syndrome of high-visibility, high-consumption foreigners bringing "wisdom" and condescension under the guise of assistance. All assistance should be offered on the basis of whether it will develop local self-management capabilities rather than whether it will necessarily produce a higher Indian GNP.

8. The United States should avoid any kind of military presence in the region, or in the Indian Ocean (except, for the near future, possibly the Persian Gulf) which would imply a significant degree of commitment to the area's defense or to the interests of one or more of the regional states. It should work for an agreement with the U.S.S.R. and, if possible, China, to win the same "self-denying" policy from them.

9. Americans must be prepared to accept national and regional strife, turbulence, and, perhaps, revolution without equating such turmoil with defeat for the American goal of a plural, self-managing, and self-defining South Asia. They must also accept the sad possibility that famine may well be inevitable given food production potential versus population increase, and that the scale of famine relief that may be necessary in the mid-1970s would exceed both the supply and the distribution capability of the U.S.

10. The United States must communicate to India that their new relationship is based on an appreciation that there can be true equality between states of great differences in material affluence. India should neither be rewarded nor scorned for its success or failure in meeting some sort of "performance criteria" in national attainment. It is to be hoped that the U.S. will view with sympathy India's own plans for itself. At the least, Washington must not insist upon its own criteria against which to measure Indian behavior. Such ethnocentric self-righteousness, often reciprocated, lies at the heart of much that is wrong with Indo-American relations.

11. By all means possible, the U.S. should encourage a Sino-Indian rapprochement to reduce both Indian defense apprehensions and Indian dependence upon the U.S.S.R.

Pakistan

For 20 years the United States has followed a policy of generous assistance to Pakistan in spite of the extreme poverty, military weakness, political disorder and negligible American economic interest in the country. This "special relationship" stemmed from an American cold war perspective and Pakistan's guileful willingness to join in a series of security agreements with the United States. By the mid-1960s, even the thin strategic justification for this relationship was in tatters, and program momentum and personal relationships were more important than national objectives. Indeed, the 1972 foreign policy message of the secretary of state noted: "We will continue our strong support for the viability and cohesion of Pakistan because of our long standing relationship and because of its importance to the stability of the entire region."[1] It would appear that a friendly policy *is* being pursued because it *has been* followed.

Pakistan's importance to the stability of the region is questionable since, in the past, its foreign and military policies have constituted the principal stimulus to change in the strategic relationships and the territorial status of the region's states. Its policies in its eastern wing produced the crisis of Bangladesh, and its leaders used military force to attempt to reopen the Kashmir dispute in 1965. In short, a strong, coherent, and viable Pakistan has not always been a stabilizing factor in South Asia.

After the dismemberment of Pakistan in 1971, its government was weak and the apparent internal cohesion of the West Pakistan provinces was tenuous. The whole of the Indus Valley is integrated by economics and transportation as well as political history and a common Muslim faith, but it is also a region of pervasive ethnic, linguistic, and sectarian rivalries. In the aftermath of the Bangladesh secession, many observers both within and outside the country feared that West Pakistan might splinter, littering the western flank of the subcontinent with unviable and unstable mini-states. This was an exaggerated fear, fueled by provincial politicians struggling for a more favorable federal division of powers and, therefore, spoils. It was labelled proto-secessionist by nationalist politicians, the army, and the central bureaucracy with the aim of centralizing power and, thus, the spoils of power.

Pakistan's leaders viewed "separatist" forces as being, at least in part, instruments of the U.S.S.R. supported by India and Afghanistan: the Soviets presumably would benefit from the creation of vulnerable states along the eastern flank of Iran and the western flank of India; the Afghans probably would be able to realize "Pukhtunistan," a Pashto-speaking state with an Arabian Sea port; the Indians would presumably like to see West Pakistan further weak-

---

[1] *United States Foreign Policy, 1972*, A Report of the Secretary of State (Washington: Government Printing Office, 1973), p. vi.

ened to forestall a future threat to India's dominion in Jammu and Kashmir. The discovery of a large number of Soviet-design machine guns in the Iraqi Embassy in Islamabad in the spring of 1973, followed within a month by the arrest of more than 30 Pakistani army officers, seemed to confirm the theory of international conspiracy for Pakistani authorities.[2]

The "Balkanization" of Pakistan, a most unlikely development, is of special concern to Iran because of its proximity and sharing of Baluchistan province and, therefore, is of concern to the United States. The same development would almost surely prove threatening to India. It would require an active Indian and/or Iranian effort to prevent Soviet or Chinese client states from being established in the subcontinent, an expensive and thankless task wholly unnecessary if Pakistan remains relatively united. Mrs. Gandhi's statements that a stable, democratic, and united West Pakistan was in the Indian interest, especially if Indo-Pakistani relations were normalized and Pakistan was "demilitarized," have to be taken as sincere.

American support for a reasonably cohesive, federal Pakistan is therefore in the interest of India and Iran, the two most important countries in the region. This support should be given, however, in such a way as to avoid developing Pakistan's military capabilities and expectations.

The strength of the military in Pakistan, in part produced by American assistance in the 1950s and 1960s,[3] was one of the factors crippling democratic development and political stability in the country, and the problem still remains. Contrary to popular Pakistani mythology, the military services do not have a monopoly of managerial or diplomatic talent, let alone probity or pragmatism, as was conclusively demonstrated in Bangladesh. Since Pakistan has almost no defense industry nor any prospect for developing it in the 1970s, its expenditures on military equipment constitute direct foreign ex-

---

[2] Leaving aside certain comic opera aspects of Iraqi bungling, most observers believed that the arms were bound for Baluchi separatists harassing the Iranian government, but perhaps with some spillover into the Pakistan-troubled part of Baluchistan. The arms discovery was coupled with the dismissal of various politicians who could hardly have been involved. Similarly, there is no public evidence to suggest that the army officer arrests were related to *provincialist* forces.

[3] Many Pakistanis believed that the U.S. rewarded the 1958 coup d'etat of General Ayub Khan. In the year after the coup, Pakistan's defense budget increased 50 percent; U.S. aid to Pakistan, however, increased 300 percent. (Defense budget, 1957-58, Rs.742.9; 1958-59, Rs.1,044.2. U.S. economic assistance, 1957-58, $61 million; 1958-59, $184 million.) See Kalim Siddiqui, *Conflict, Crisis and War in Pakistan* (London: Macmillan, 1972), pp. 95-100.

change costs of no social or economic benefit, and have no significant effect on military relationships vis-à-vis India (which is too large) or Afghanistan (which is too small). Arms assistance and sales, however, fortify the officer corps against competing Pakistani groups interested in development, savings, or social investment. In any case, a high proportion of the defense budget represents consumption by the officer corps at an unconscionable level in a country as poor as Pakistan.

It is unlikely that the United States can change this situation appreciably, but it should follow policies which do not stand in the way of other Pakistani groups doing so over a period of time. This can best be accomplished by a realization that the army does not constitute a stabilizing force within the country. If law and order concerns bring forward a request for assistance from Islamabad, Washington should assist the police rather than the army.

While supplying spare parts for American equipment may be the least expensive way of satisfying the minimum force needs of the Pakistani services, such assistance should be clearly tied to defense planning which reduces or at least freezes military spending levels. U.S. "normalization" and economic assistance ought to serve this same goal; what Pakistan receives in foreign concessional assistance ought not to further the unnecessary, wasteful, and destabilizing growth of military expenditures. Without such American pressure (and perhaps even with it), Pakistan's leaders will find it almost impossible to resist military demands based on an inflated appetite inherited from the past, justified by Indian strength, and informed by a dream of a Pakistani Kashmir.

American arms policy must also be accompanied by an implicit American acceptance of the Simla agreement in which Kashmir is henceforth considered to be a bilateral matter. The U.S. has no interest in a particular settlement of the dispute, which has poisoned relations between the two countries and led to disastrous wars. Kashmir has been a heavy burden to India, both to its democratic values and its public exchequer, and to Pakistan, dazzling it with dreams of a bygone era and dividing its public men as has no other issue.[4] A settlement of the dispute seems wholly unlikely, but if it does materialize it will be by Indo-Pakistani agreement. The United States should accept this position in its own stance and pronounce-

---

[4] In Siddiqui's phrase, "The story of Pakistan-Indian relations is a story of two shattered, incomplete, self-images each trying to restore itself at the expense of the other." *Conflict, Crisis and War in Pakistan*, p. 158. This is much more descriptive of Pakistan than India.

ments, and leave aside judgments about the merits in the case—the true merits lie in burying the dispute.

Pakistan's claim for economic assistance, shorn of anachronistic strategic calculations, is strong. The nature of the country requires it to follow a development model based on high levels of world trade and integration, and foreign exchange availability is therefore crucial. Pakistan has to import technology, skills, and resources, and its agriculture-based exports therefore have to be produced with high efficiency.

Past performance seems to indicate that Pakistani economic managers and entrepreneurs are extremely able, at least under conditions of high levels of concessional assistance. The "green revolution" in agriculture, especially wheat, and excellent cotton land have given the economy a buoyant phase at the key moment when the loss of East Pakistan led to massive dislocations. Foreign assistance to the "new" Pakistan should further develop the economy with large measures of foreign trade. The shortage of cereals for P.L. 480 shipment may also help Pakistan create incentives for agricultural production.

Pakistan remains a woefully poor country, however, and the prospects for an agriculture-led, high growth rate economy are not bright. As with India, Pakistan's aspirations must be scaled down to the near-term potentials of a slightly increased standard of living, a qualitative improvement in social services and cultural activity, and a more relevant and achievable notion of "the good life." High growth, in fact, is necessary merely to keep pace with population growth and provide even a modest amount of capital for long-term productive and social investment.

In sum, American foreign policy toward Pakistan might usefully follow these lines:

1. An explicit recognition that Pakistan's best interests lie with a strategic accommodation with India and an end to the Kashmir dispute.

2. A stated commitment to the need for reduced or at least "frozen" levels of military expenditure as a prerequisite to arms sales and to high levels of economic assistance.

3. Continuing pressure on other members of the Aid-Pakistan Consortium to provide more support, to include Pakistan in the Asian Development Bank area, and to support Pakistan's position in the trading world by a development use of SDRs and preferential trading rights.

4. The rescheduling or forgiving of some of Pakistan's external bilateral debt to the United States as part of future economic assistance.

5. The encouragement of American manufacturing firms to invest in Pakistan, especially in nontraditional sectors, with guarantees that would make such investment as attractive as that in richer countries.

6. United States technical assistance to Pakistan should emphasize the strengthening of local institutions and training centers rather than the foreign training of personnel which has tended to promote emigration or alienation.

7. The United States should encourage Pakistani-Iranian joint ventures in economics and in culture wherever possible, and it should support the Regional Cooperation for Development organization as a viable instrument of regional integration and cooperation.

8. The United States should be prepared to accept a high level of political tension and assertion in the country, and possibly between it and its neighbors. Unless there is convincing evidence of Soviet or Chinese attempts to dominate or divide the country, the U.S. should maintain a distant, neutral position on questions of the security of the Pakistani state and not participate in its militarization.

9. The special historical ties between the United States and Pakistan should be gently reduced. Pakistan's sense of self-reliance must be encouraged, and false dependencies must be discouraged. This will be difficult to accomplish both in Islamabad and in Washington.

10. Pakistan should be discouraged from thinking of itself as "gateway to the Persian Gulf" or as an Indian Ocean power. These are slogans with neither military nor economic relevance, and they would tend to distract both the U.S. and Pakistan from establishing normal diplomatic relations.

Bangladesh

At least in economic terms, Bangladesh is the least viable of the South Asian countries, largely because of the very unfavorable man/land ratio and the precarious cultivation conditions in the lower Ganges Delta. In no other country in the world are the odds against a successful transition to self-sustaining economic growth and a demographically stable society greater.

There are three possibilities for a country like Bangladesh: widespread anarchy, disorder, and famine, with the cities remaining "viable" only through international relief; a relatively stable if un-satisfactory standard of living, with a growth in services and social organization; and integration into a larger Indian economy with more opportunity for specialization.

Of these "alternatives," the second is most likely, and in terms of the Awami League leadership's values, the most desirable. The first alternative is a possibility, although not perhaps a great one in the 1970s. Most observers believe that with better water management and continued economic assistance from the world, Bangladesh's pro-duction can keep pace (or almost keep pace) with population growth. Even if it did not, famine would presumably strike the least organized and most remote elements of the population, and this would not necessarily weaken either the state as a whole or the urban area. This eventually might require authoritarian measures and capacities, but they would probably originate from the "right" rather than the "left." The region's poverty will doubtless not be equitably shared, but there are few centers of privilege in East Bengal. Land holdings are small and fragmented; there is no indigenous entrepreneurial group; the means of production, such as they are, are either nation-alized or very small in scale.

The possibility of integration into India, no matter how attrac-tive economically, is unlikely because of Bangladeshi nationalism and a residual anti-Hindu sentiment. Pre-1947 Bengal was a society in which the Hindus were dominant, and few Bangladeshis would want to return to that kind of world. The imperatives for greater coopera-tion, however, ought not to be ignored. Water management in the Ganges Valley should be a matter for Indo-Bangladeshi cooperation; so should jute marketing. Bangladesh represents an agricultural hinterland to Calcutta, and increasing agricultural production could find a ready market there, just as Calcutta's industrial products are both relevant and "priced right" for Bangladesh. In addition, of course, Bangladesh shares history, language, and culture with western Bengal.

American foreign policy toward Bangladesh, in the first instance properly humanitarian and compassionate, requires a decision as to whether it is in the interest of the United States to serve the "national-ist" or the "integrationist" aspects of the new state's life. The former is more conventional, and would be preferred in Dacca and, perhaps, New Delhi as well. It would not, however, best serve many of the basic economic and social needs of the residents of Bangladesh. At present, there is a large scale "illegal" flow of goods, services, and people across the indistinct Indo-Bangladeshi frontier. In addition,

India and Bangladesh find themselves competing for a small and declining jute market, and Bangladesh must import its industrial goods from high-cost countries whereas India has underutilized capacity.

The optimum policy would appear to be one under which Bangladesh sovereignty was acknowledged and its political independence encouraged, while its economy was influenced to develop joint enterprises with that of India. This might be welcomed in New Delhi, would be only slightly distasteful to Dacca, and would provide capital, skills, and markets to Bangladesh's infant economy for the 1970s.

Bangladesh poses a security problem to no country, nor does it represent a major prize in the competition between the great powers. Its own defense is almost entirely dependent upon India—an arrangement that should be encouraged. China's involvement in local politics has been undercut by many factors: the Pakistani army's assault on leftists as well as nationalists in the civil war, the attention paid pro-Chinese groups in Bangladesh by the Indian army and intelligence services during the occupation period, and the Awami League's root-and-branch attack on its rivals since independence. The pro-Chinese forces were never large, and if any still exist, have no access to Peking since there are no relations between the two states.

The Soviet role, which appeared to be ambitious in the first instance, was reduced to that of a large international donor soon after independence. Moscow was doubtless aware that New Delhi would resent any major steps toward building up the Soviet presence, and not even the Russians could find many interests to advance in Bangladesh unless they could establish facilities there. Thus when the Russian offer to clear the port of Khulna (as well as Chittagong harbor) was sent back to the U.S.S.R. with a request for a more prompt schedule of work, the Russians churlishly dropped the project entirely.

The pro-Soviet Communists are presumably slightly less ravaged than the pro-Peking faction, but are in any case a small force. The Soviets have little interest in counseling a miniscule political group to lay siege to a friendly government, especially if it would cost Indian friendship. In short, Bangladesh is an Indian protectorate that benefits from its relative unimportance in world politics and its distance from any major revisionist power. This set of conditions favors the limitation of expenditures on military forces.

An optimum American foreign policy toward Bangladesh would have the following attributes:

1. The United States should continue rehabilitation and emergency relief assistance to stabilize food availability and restore farm-to-market transportation systems.

2. There should be an emphasis on multilateral economic assistance efforts, with as large a measure of grants and donations as possible. The U.S. can facilitate this development by forgiving that percentage of Bangladesh-assumed development loans which were a casualty of the war and rescheduling debt repayments for a remainder of the portion assigned to Bangladesh by aid donors.

3. An agreement should be concluded with the government of India providing that some U.S.-owned Indian currency could be used for Bangladesh assistance, especially for those categories of Indian production in which there is underutilized capacity. There is a parallel to this recommendation in the U.S. aid program for Nepal which, while not without its problems, has some benefits.

4. Future development assistance in the manufacturing sector should be given with an incentive for Indo-Bangladeshi joint production and marketing.

5. Technical assistance and the use of U.S.-owned local currency should emphasize social and institutional development as well as directly productive capital projects. The emigration of trained manpower to the U.S. and to international organizations should be discouraged because of the shortage of skilled technical manpower in the country.

6. U.S. officials and experts in-country should be as few as possible, and all authority should be vested in Bangladeshi officials and groups. Probably most of the essential skills exist in the country; a tradition of responsible self-management is what has been missing, and must be developed by experience.

7. The United States should undertake no consultations on defense or military supply with Dacca, and if asked should encourage it to seek collaboration with New Delhi.

8. The tone of American policy ought to be sympathetic and supportive, but neither U.S. interests nor resources favor an intimate U.S.-Bangladesh relationship. The best medium for the development effort would be a multilateral lending organization with the U.S. in a relatively modest profile.

9. As with the other countries in South Asia, U.S. policy makers and the public must expect and accept political turbulence, economic distress and, sadly, human devastation. There is no way any external power can adequately assist or identify the proper future configuration

of power in a society so utterly different from its own. There is no immediate possibility of the world's resources being adequate to meet Bangladeshi population growth rates which may be in excess of 3 percent a year, and there is no technology by which starving people scattered in a riverine delta can be delivered the food necessary to support life if their own labor cannot accomplish that on their soil. What must be developed are the centers from which greater growth and greater human expression can be sustained and which can survive a localized famine. Development assistance to Bangladesh must, therefore, make such gains as may be possible in agriculture and then look to urban centers as the hope of the future.

Conclusion

The opportunities for a new, creative American foreign policy in South Asia are at hand, but its resources, approaches and rationale must be significantly changed from those of the past. A greater reliance upon local views, institutions, and aspirations must take a greater precedence in the U.S. decision-making process. The direct commitment of American personnel and resources must be greatly reduced, and conserved for those problems in which there is neither international accord nor superpower agreement, and, hence, which are competitive and inherently burdensome.

In areas like South Asia, there are enormous resources, and development must be seen as the process by which indigenous resources are increasingly mobilized and shaped. "Development by transfer" is an outmoded concept; "assistance for self-management" must replace it as the rationale of a smaller and more sophisticated American aid diplomacy.

South Asia is relatively fortunate in its strategic placement and in the equilibrium being established by the great powers. The realities of the concentration of power place India at the apex of the security system in the region, but with domestic constraints that limit its foreign capabilities and aspirations. Pakistan has the capacity to manage its own society but not to contest for Kashmir, and that realization should allow a redirection of resource allocation that offers the country its best chance for security and independence. Bangladesh is in fact a "quasi-protectorate," which might also be an advantageous position for it to accept, especially since it can do so implicitly. For the 1970s, unless there are very great changes indeed, South Asia can be considered, for American purposes, to be a zone of peace, and hence, one in which the official presence can be reduced according to a model that sees U.S. policy solely as "facilitative assistance."